ENOUGH!

CENTER FOR THE STUDY
OF GUN VIOLENCE

Center for the Study of Gun Violence
Lake Worth, Florida 33467

http://thomasgaborbooks.com

ISBN (print): 978-1-7336908-0-5
ISBN (eBook): 978-1-7336908-1-2

Ordering Information:

Special discounts are available on quantity purchases by corporations,
associations, and others. For details, contact the author at
tgaborauthor@gmail.com.

ENOUGH!

Solving America's Gun Violence Crisis

THOMAS GABOR

Consultant And Expert Witness
Professor of Criminology
(Retired, University of Ottawa)

To the victims of gun violence and their families,
as well as the activists, researchers, and healers
working to alleviate the suffering from this scourge.

TABLE OF CONTENTS

PART V: CITIZEN INITIATIVES

PART VI: POLICY LESSONS FROM THE FIELD

Preface

There are nearly 40,000 gun-related deaths each year in the United States. Every 18 months, the number of Americans who die from gunshot wounds equals the number who perished throughout the entire Vietnam War! Yet, rather than holding the massive protests seen against that war, the country as a whole has been far more restrained in its reaction to gun violence. Despite the annual death toll and almost daily mass shootings, many Americans feel helpless and unable to take action. We also are condemned by human rights groups, such as Amnesty International, which accuse the US of committing human rights violations by failing to protect its own citizens from gun violence.

In America, "the right to live free from violence, discrimination and fear has been superseded by a sense of entitlement to own a practically unlimited array of deadly weapons, without sufficient regulations on their acquisition, possession and use,"[1] the organization concluded in a September 2018 report.

Despite such condemnations, the seemingly endless carnage and a litany of bad news, I'm hopeful that significant change will occur in the next 10 years. Here's why:

1. Gun ownership in the US has been declining since the 1970s. The University of Chicago's National Opinion Research Center has shown that in 2010 and 2014 about 32 percent of adults lived in households with firearms. In 1976 to 1982, 51 percent of adults lived in households with one or more guns.[2]

2. Public opinion has been shifting in the last few years in favor of stricter gun laws. About nine in 10

Americans favor expanding background checks to all firearm sales.

3. A large grassroots movement to counter the gun lobby and effect major change has been growing since the 2012 mass shooting of children at Sandy Hook Elementary School in Newtown (Connecticut). After another mass casualty shooting at Marjory Stoneman Douglas High School in Parkland (Florida) six years later, the growth of the gun violence prevention movement has accelerated with numerous marches, more lobbying, and a much larger number of volunteers nationally.

4. The National Rifle Association's economic strength and political influence are in decline. The gun industry is experiencing a drop in sales and facing opposition from groups on the upswing, such as Everytown for Gun Safety and former Congresswoman Gabrielle Giffords' organization. The NRA also is facing damage to its image due to serious allegations that it colluded with Russia to help Donald Trump, an NRA-friendly candidate, win the presidency in 2016.

5. In the 2018 midterm elections, anti-gun violence groups outspent the NRA, and many candidates calling for stricter gun regulations prevailed. Candidates are no longer so afraid of the NRA's influence that they refuse to discuss gun violence and prioritize gun policy.

6. The voters of the future are youth, and they tend to support more restrictive gun laws because they feel threatened by gun violence.

One significant challenge has little to do with public opinion, grassroots mobilization, or the state of the gun business. The challenge is that of an electoral system that gives rural voters a disproportionate voice over city dwellers, allows voter suppression aimed at minority groups that are more supportive of gun regulations, and that enables special interests to shape election outcomes. These issues need to be addressed if the voice of the majority on guns is to be heard.

I owe a great debt to so many people and groups with whom I have exchanged views or who have inspired me over the last few years. Experts, such as David Hemenway of Harvard University, Jamie Fox of Northeastern University, and Stephen Teret, Professor Emeritus of Johns Hopkins University provided valuable feedback and encouragement related to my previous book, *Confronting Gun Violence in America*. The late Maurice Murad, an award-winning producer at *60 Minutes*, believed that my book made an enormous contribution to debunking many of the NRA's talking points with hard data. Mike Weisser (a.k.a. Mike the Gun Guy), an expert on guns and the gun business, has challenged my views by asking the tough questions about the practicality of some of the solutions I advocate.

I'm also indebted to my many friends and groups on Facebook with whom I exchange views on a regular basis. Ladd Everitt of One Pulse for America, Marji Hope of WAAR, Palm Beach Indivisibles, Women's March of Florida, Repeal the Second Amendment, Gays Against Guns, and many others have been highly supportive and often shared my posts. Rose Rowland, who facilitates an online gun violence book club, selected my book last year for their discussions and helped spread my message advocating the establishment of a national licensing system for gun owners. Also, I had the opportunity to address many audiences at churches and synagogues (including a group of atheists!), community centers, concerts, panels, rallies, and meetings of various gun safety groups and non-profit organizations.

Many fellow peace warriors in the gun violence prevention movement have been accidental activists, committed to the cause after they survived a gun attack or catastrophic personal loss. Angela Williams, founder of Mothers Against Murderers Association in West Palm Beach (Florida) has lost 14 family members to gun violence and attended hundreds of funerals in her community. Former Congresswoman Giffords of Tucson (Arizona) survived an assassination attempt in which 18 other people were shot and eventually formed a group with her husband, Mark Kelly, dedicated to the prevention of gun violence. Sandy Anglin Phillips and her husband, Lonnie, who lost their beloved daughter, Jessi, in the Aurora (Colorado) theater shooting, have been motivated by their personal tragedy to support and empower survivors around the country.

I also have had the opportunity to meet many intelligent, committed, and dynamic leaders who are trying to make a difference in gun policy. My friend, Barry Silver, both an attorney and a rabbi, is a relentless agent for change, as are the many interfaith groups he leads. The ubiquitous Moms Demand Action for Gun Sense in America, the largest grassroots organization in the country, offers great hope. I know that at the end of the day their desire for a life free of violence for their children will supersede any zealot's love for his guns. My affiliation with the League of Women Voters also has brought me into contact with many dedicated volunteers from the state to local levels in Florida. I also served on panels with student leaders from Parkland and met their family members.

This book is dedicated to the activists who are battling gun violence at so many levels throughout the country. As I strive to make my own contribution by laying out a road map for change in America, I am especially grateful for the love, partnership, and support of my beloved wife, Christene.

Thomas Gabor, Ph.D., Palm Beach County, Florida, 2019

1

America's Gun Violence Crisis

America is engulfed by gun violence, testing the sense of security of its people as they go about their daily lives. The United States has 5 percent of the world's population but experiences a third of the planet's mass shootings.[3] The gun homicide rate is 25 times the combined rate of other high-income countries.[4] With nearly one school shooting a week, the US had 288 school shootings from January 2009 through May 2018.[5] No other G7 (major industrialized) country has had more than two school shootings during that nine-year period. Every 18 months, civilian gun deaths in America equal those of US military personnel during the entire Vietnam war.

These numbers are perhaps not surprising given the level of gun ownership in the US. A recent international survey showed that there are now approximately 393 million privately-held firearms in the US (120 firearms for every 100 people), more than five times that of India, a country with the next largest civilian arsenal and four times America's population.[6]

Gun violence takes more than a physical toll on its victims. Millions of American women have been threatened or shot at by an intimate partner, and the psychological impact of abuse is magnified when guns are involved.[7] Bystanders to violence also may be profoundly affected. A health team assessing witnesses to a mass shooting in Killeen, Texas, in the 1990s found that 28 percent met the criteria for posttraumatic stress disorder one month after the incident.[8] A year later, 18 percent still suffered from PTSD. Few had no symptoms of posttraumatic stress. Even those not present at a shooting may be affected emotionally. An American Psychological Association survey has found that for 15- to 21-year-olds, mass shootings constitute the greatest source of stress, with three out of four feeling stressed about the possibility of encountering a mass or school shooting.[9]

Consider the impact of a mass shooting on the friend of a victim who was not even living in the same town. Jessica Ghawi, a 24-year-old aspiring sportscaster, was murdered in 2012 during the mass shooting at the Century Theater in Aurora, Colorado. Just prior to the sixth anniversary of the shooting, her best friend posted the following on Facebook:

> *In 22 days, it will mark the six year anniversary of when my best friend was murdered with 11 others, and 58 others injured from gun violence. The panic attacks haven't stopped. A few months ago, I had a panic attack on the way to my nephew's birthday celebration that was so severe, my sister had to leave her son, on his birthday, to come save me on the side of the highway because I didn't know how to breathe.*
>
> *The nightmares haven't stopped. I have dreams on a weekly, sometimes daily basis, that involve mass shootings or gun violence. The PTSD hasn't stopped. I was diagnosed*

in 2018, this year, with PTSD due to the trauma I experienced from my best friend's horrific murder.

Six years. And I wasn't even there when Jessi was murdered. I was over 900 miles away. I can't even begin to imagine the trauma of actually experiencing a mass shooting. My heart hurts. I'm tired of posting the names of those murdered in mass shootings. I'm tired of reliving the trauma. I am tired of thinking about the pain that those families are feeling, the pain I felt almost six years ago, the pain that they will continue to feel for years to come...

Gun violence disproportionately touches the African-American community because murder, often involving guns, is the most frequent cause of death among black males between the ages of 15 and 34.[10] However, the varied locations of recent mass shootings—schools, colleges, night clubs, concerts, places of worship, movie theaters, malls, airports, banks, even a yoga studio—shows that no one is immune from this scourge.

Nor is this a problem exclusive to inner cities. Many mass shootings occur in suburbs and small towns, many shooters are white, and several states without a major city (e.g., Alaska, Montana) rank high in terms of gun death rates.[11] While this issue is often treated as a partisan concern of "liberals," all segments of society are vulnerable. Bullets don't distinguish between Democrats, Republicans, and Independents, and many smaller communities have a significant problem.

While Australia, New Zealand, Germany, Canada, and the United Kingdom have introduced major changes to their gun laws following high profile mass shootings, the US has failed to pass a significant gun law at the federal level for more than 25 years, despite a surge in mass shootings, especially since 2007. Laws at the state level have been as likely to loosen gun restrictions as to tighten them, including making it easier to carry guns and, in a quarter of the states, eliminating required permits to carry guns. Stand Your Ground laws enable the use of lethal force, without a duty to retreat, when an individual *feels* that his life is threatened. The effects of such laws have been devastating, increasing homicide rates in states adopting them.

In addition, a growing number of states allow guns to be carried openly and brought into settings such as bars, college campuses, and even government buildings. More than 40 states have enacted broad preemption statutes that tie the hands of local officials by preventing counties and municipalities from passing their own gun laws. Local laws, while complicating enforcement, may be warranted due to differences in attitudes and population density, especially between rural communities and urban centers.

While some tightening of laws also has occurred at the state level, the gun lobby and its supporters tend to vigorously resist even modest changes. For example, after the mass shooting at Marjory Stoneman Douglas High School in Parkland, legislators refused to consider a ban on assault-style weapons or closing the private sale loophole that allows about a quarter of gun transfers to occur without any criminal background checks of buyers. Relatively small proposed changes, such as raising the age requirement to 21 for a gun purchase, were met with a vow by Marion Hammer, the National Rifle Association's chief lobbyist in Florida, to punish lawmakers who had supported these measures. In a post on the website AmmoLand, Ms. Hammer called out 17 Republican legislators who supported the reforms, labeling them "turncoats" and no longer worthy of the support of the NRA or gun rights advocates.[12]

I propose a bold agenda in this book. At speaking engagements, I often have been asked to speculate as to whether certain solutions to gun violence are achievable, such as the licensing of gun owners or the banning of military-style weapons. My response is that the political environment is not static and reforms we cannot envision today may be very doable in the near future. Who would have expected Australia, a country with a frontier heritage and strong gun lobby, to melt down up to a third of all its firearms after their horrific mass shooting in 1996? Who would have expected the call for gun policy reforms in the US to be led by high school kids from Florida who have just seen their school attacked by a troubled young man with an assault rifle? In my view, the worst thing we can do is to so water down our proposals to accommodate anticipated resistance that the measures we ultimately adopt fail to save lives. Imagine if all the energy, money, lobbying, and political capital spent to pass a bill fails to enhance public safety and merely discredits efforts to regulate firearms and the industry that produces and sells them.

My role is to put solutions that have worked before the American people and to make the strongest case for them. Then, it is up to my fellow citizens to decide on the reforms they will support. I bring a uniquely international perspective to this issue, having spent my early years in Europe, received an education in the United States and Canada, worked as a Professor of Criminology in Canada, served as an adviser to the United Nations and many government agencies, and as an expert witness to Lord Cullen's inquiry in the UK following a massacre of elementary school children in Dunblane, Scotland. I have undertaken research in the area of gun violence for 30 years. Most researchers in the area have a public health background rather than one in the interdisciplinary field of criminology.

Public opinion polls show that most Americans support many forms of gun regulation. A national survey in April 2018 found that 52 percent of Americans wanted stricter gun laws to be the top legislative priority in Congress, and another 19 percent stated it should be a priority but not the top priority.[13] Just a quarter of Americans said that gun legislation should not be a priority. This survey also found that Americans who believe that it is more important to control gun violence (57 percent) outnumber those who believe that it is more important to protect gun rights (38 percent). In addition, the poll showed that a majority of Americans favor a ban on semiautomatic assault weapons and that 86 percent would cast a ballot for a candidate who called for an expansion of background checks to cover private gun sales. There are indications that public opinion has shifted in favor of a bolder approach toward guns.[14]

In addition, a 2017 national poll conducted on behalf of the Johns Hopkins Bloomberg School of Public Health showed that the divide between gun owners and non-gun owners is not as wide as commonly believed.[15] Policies receiving strong support from both groups included:

- Universal background checks
- License suspension for gun dealers who cannot account for 20 or more guns in their inventory
- Higher safety training standards for individuals holding concealed-carry permits
- Better reporting of mental health records for background checks
- Gun prohibitions for people subject to temporary domestic violence restraining orders
- Gun violence restraining orders.

Also encouraging is that national groups promoting public safety outspent the NRA in the midterm elections, including Giffords (cofounded by former Congresswoman Gabrielle Giffords, who was wounded in a 2011 mass shooting) and Everytown for Gun Safety. These groups also helped a number of "gun sense" candidates win elections or helped defeat incumbents with high NRA ratings.[16] These groups are now serving as a political counterweight to the NRA.

As for the idea that laws restricting gun ownership violate the Second Amendment, US courts have consistently upheld the types of legislative reforms recommended in this book. More than 90 percent of the challenges to gun laws since the landmark 2008 *Heller* decision have failed to overturn these laws, despite the fact that this ruling for the first time recognized an individual's right to gun ownership outside of militia service.[17] Courts are therefore not striking down most gun laws, and this is consistent with the Heller ruling which made it clear that:

> *Like most rights, the Second Amendment right is not unlimited. It is not a right to keep and carry any weapon whatsoever in any manner whatsoever and for whatever purpose: For example, concealed weapons prohibitions have been upheld under the Amendment or state analogues. The Court's opinion should not be taken to cast doubt on longstanding prohibitions on the possession of firearms by felons and the mentally ill, or laws forbidding the carrying of firearms in sensitive places such as schools and government buildings, or laws imposing conditions and qualifications on the commercial sale of arms. Miller's [previous Court ruling] holding that the sorts of weapons protected are those "in common use at the time" finds supporting the historical tradition of prohibiting the carrying of dangerous and unusual weapons.[18]*

As far as public safety is concerned, a growing body of research has shown that overly permissive laws, more guns and gun carrying, and lax gun storage tend to result in more firearm deaths and injuries. The reader can examine this body of evidence in my 2016 book, *Confronting Gun Violence in America.*[19]

Public opinion, research, and current interpretations of the Constitution all support efforts aiming to adopt stricter measures in relation to guns. Failing to act is not an option since our continuing rates of gun violence and parade of mass shootings will lead to increasing levels of fear and distrust. Our nation's children are afraid to go to school due to their fear of a mass shooting. The financial costs of gun violence have been estimated at more than $200 billion per year when the costs of direct medical care, rehabilitation, victims' lost income, criminal justice system expenditures, security, and lost quality of life are considered.[20]

The gun lobby sees itself as a champion of freedom. While they may champion the freedom of a small minority to own any type of firearm, including military-style firearms, our continuing failure to regulate firearms sufficiently undermines the freedoms of Americans in many ways. Without a significant response, the near daily mass shootings and the significant number of gun deaths each year will erode personal freedoms.

We are seeing more calls for armed security and an increased law enforcement presence following mass shootings in schools, college campuses, airports, night clubs, and other venues in which large-scale atrocities have occurred. Children and youth who are terrified to go to school and traumatized by active shooter drills do not feel freer. More law enforcement surveillance of public areas represents an erosion of our privacy, rather than more freedom. Having our bags checked and being scanned before we enter buildings, malls, and stadiums also will limit our freedoms. Allowing guns on college campuses inhibits rather than encourages the open discussion of controversial topics. Allowing guns at protests certainly stifles free expression on the part of those being intimidated. Pandering to a vocal and aggressive minority concerned only about their gun rights will undermine American freedom and democracy.

Overview of the Book

Gun violence solutions recommended in this book are presented in several sections. Part I discusses the most effective means of regulating gun ownership, including an argument and proposal for creating a national licensing system for gun owners. Part I also covers gun carrying regulations and policies to keep guns from individuals who pose an elevated risk of committing acts of violence and to prevent unauthorized access to guns through safe storage.

Part II deals with regulating weapons, especially those capable of mass casualty incidents. In addition, one chapter addresses the development and commercial sale of personalized or smart weapons, which can reduce unauthorized access and prevent incidents involving children and youth. Part III calls for increased regulation of the gun industry, including the removal of legal barriers that protect the industry from liability for gun-related injuries and deaths. This section also discusses the need to have increased oversight over gun dealers and to ensure that guns are subject to consumer protections to avoid the dangers posed by guns of inferior design or quality.

Part IV addresses the need to change violent norms by repealing laws that encourage violence (e.g. Stand Your Ground), deterring individual and gang violence, interrupting retaliatory violence, and assisting those at high risk of violence to tackle personal issues (employment, education, substance abuse, mental health) so they will take a different path. Part V discusses what ordinary citizens can do to make communities safer with respect to gun violence. Aside from changing laws regulating gun owners, firearms, the industry, and cracking down on the most violent individuals, there are many voluntary initiatives (e.g. gun buybacks) and nongovernmental efforts, including raising awareness, consumer activism, and community mobilization.

Part VI provides two important policy lessons based on the research and experience with school shootings and suicide. This section underscores the importance of a comprehensive approach to preventing gun violence rather than a single factor approach focusing exclusively on improving the security of schools and other vulnerable targets. At the same time, experience with suicide makes the point that a comprehensive approach to any form of gun-related injury must recognize that weapons matter and that the accessibility of firearms must be part of any comprehensive strategy to prevent violent attacks or suicide attempts.

A concluding section calls for more research on gun violence after funding has been suppressed by members of Congress acting on behalf of a powerful gun lobby. It calls for us not to accept the present situation as normal and to reject the NRA's debunked narrative that guns serve to make our homes and communities safer. This narrative serves the commercial interests of the gun industry and a small uncompromising minority of gun owners.

In a final section, I present a draft of the *Declaration of Rights and Resolutions in Relation to Gun Violence.* Such a *Declaration* recognizes the fact that living free of gun violence has been recognized as a human right. In addition, it can serve as a counterpoint to the Second Amendment. Yes, gun owners have certain rights, although these rights have been greatly distorted and exaggerated. However, it is my view that the majority of citizens who do not own guns and owners who are concerned about public safety need to assert their rights to live in peace and without the constant fear of being shot. I welcome the reader's feedback on this *Declaration* and how it ought to be promoted.

Part I

Regulating Gun Ownership

2

Licensing Owners to Replace a Broken Background Check System

The National Instant Criminal Background Check System (NICS) was designed to ensure that individuals purchasing guns through a licensed dealer do not fall into a prohibited category and can lawfully acquire a firearm. Currently, someone with a felony record, a fugitive from justice, an individual with a history of domestic violence or mental illness, a minor, someone using prohibited drugs, or a person dishonorably discharged from the military cannot legally purchase a firearm from a gun dealer. However, about 25 percent of gun sales or transfers occur privately through gun shows, online, or through personal networks and require no background checks at all. That means anyone falling in one of the prohibited categories can obtain guns through a legal channel. They do not need to buy guns from gun traffickers for cash on the street. This is the loophole that nine in 10 Americans would like to close, and that would be a good thing.

However, even without this loophole, NICS suffers from some very serious and probably fatal flaws. Simply closing a loophole is a band-aid for a system that should be abandoned altogether and replaced by one that performs a thorough screening of anybody who wants to buy a product that is designed to kill. Many mass shooters have passed NICS checks, including: Stephen Paddock, who shot close to five hundred people at a Las Vegas concert; Omar Mateen, who shot over one hundred people at the Orlando Pulse nightclub; Nikolas Cruz, who shot and killed 17 students and staff at a high school in Parkland; Dylann Roof, who murdered nine people at the Emanuel African Methodist Episcopal Church in Charleston, South Carolina; Robert Bowers, who murdered 11 worshippers at a Pittsburgh synagogue; and Devin Kelley, who murdered 26 people at a church in Sutherland Springs, Texas.

How can this happen? When a sale is conducted through a licensed firearm dealer, the FBI is contacted by phone or online or, in some states, through a state agency that serves as the point of contact. Three FBI databases are searched in about one to two minutes. If no matches are found to a criminal record or other disqualifying factor, the dealer is told to proceed with the transaction. If these searches yield a match with criminal, mental health, drug, or domestic violence records, a further investigation averaging eight minutes is conducted by a NICS examiner. The examiner then advises the licensed dealer to proceed, deny, or delay the transaction. In the case of a delay, the transaction proceeds by default after three business days if disqualifying information is not found by the FBI. This happened in the case of Dylann Roof, the South Carolina church shooter, because the search did not uncover a previous drug conviction. He was then able to purchase the Glock pistol he used to kill pastor and state Senator Clementa Pinckney and eight others during Bible study.

The NICS system also is plagued by the lack of verification of declarations made by purchasers/transferees. The Bureau of Alcohol, Tobacco, Firearms and Explosives (ATF) Form 4473 asks the buyer to respond to questions such as whether they use an illegal substance, have been convicted of a felony, dishonorably discharged from the military, or hospitalized for a mental illness. This information often cannot be verified because the FBI relies on the states and military to share information with the Bureau, and states are not required to gather and share information on state crimes and mental health records. In any event, three days is not a lot of time for the FBI to do much beyond searching their databases. In the 2017 church shooting in Sutherland Springs, the shooter's record of domestic violence in the military, which would have disqualified him from buying guns, was not shared by the US Air Force.

NICS appears to have a fatal flaw due to legal challenges that have exposed the inherent limitations of the electronic records used in conducting a background check. Here is a brief explanation. In 1993, President Clinton signed into law the *Brady Handgun Violence Prevention Act,* which established a system to determine whether firearm buyers fell into a prohibited category by virtue of a felony record, mental illness, dishonorable discharge from the military, or other disqualification. Before the system took effect in 1998, interim procedures were established requiring local law enforcement agencies to make a reasonable effort within five days to ascertain whether the acquisition of a firearm by a prospective transferee was in violation of the *Brady Act*. State and county agencies were instructed to search state and local records as part of the process.

Sheriffs in Montana and Arizona challenged this requirement and, following split decisions in the courts, the US Supreme Court in *Printz v. United States* ruled that on Tenth Amendment grounds state resources could not be commandeered by the federal government to conduct background checks.[21] As a result, the NICS system cannot count on the states to forward state criminal and mental health records to the FBI system, making it a voluntary system with varying cooperation across states.

A variety of sources have revealed that many states are not forwarding critical information to the FBI. A report by the Government Accountability Office points to bureaucratic and technical barriers, like switching from paper-based to computer systems. Some states also contend it violates their laws to forward mental health records to the federal database.[22] Most states are not providing noncriminal records, such as those related to positive drug test results for persons on probation. As of May 1, 2012, Department of Justice data showed that 30 states were not making any noncriminal records available.

The Giffords Law Center notes that federal law "cannot require states to make information identifying people ineligible to possess firearms available to the federal or state agencies that perform background checks, and many states fail to voluntarily report the necessary records to the proper databases. As a result, the information that is searched during a background check is often incomplete."[23] The center adds that the problem of incomplete and inconsistent reporting from the states applies to all records, including criminal history, mental health, drug abuse, domestic violence, juvenile, and protective order records. As a result, there is underreporting of records related to every category of person prohibited from possessing firearms.

A 2011 report by Mayors Against Illegal Guns (MAIG) identified "fatal gaps" in the background check system that contributed to high-profile mass shootings such as the one at Virginia Tech and the Tucson shooting in which Rep. Giffords was nearly assassinated.[24] This study found that incomplete reporting of mental health and drug records was especially problematic. It found that nearly half the states, as well as the District of Columbia, reported fewer than 100 mental health records and several reported none. Forty-four states submitted fewer than 10 records to the controlled substance file in the NICS Index and 33 states submitted no records at all. While federal regulations and policies established that a failed drug test, single drug-related arrest, or admission of drug use within the past year should temporarily disqualify someone from possessing a gun, the vast majority of states were unaware that these records should be shared with NICS.

Perhaps even more disconcerting was the finding that federal agencies often fail to share mental health records. MAIG's report showed that 52 of 61 agencies reported no mental health records to NICS. In addition, most federal agencies have not submitted substance abuse records. A lack of awareness of reporting requirements, inadequate funding, and poor enforcement of noncompliance with federal regulations all contributed to this state of affairs.

An inherent limitation of the background check system is the comprehensiveness of electronic databases designed to capture criminal behavior. Every introductory criminology student knows that an individual's formal criminal record represents just a fraction of his or her lawbreaking. No crime is detected and reported 100 percent of the time, and many serious offenses, such as rape, domestic assault, and sex offenses against children are rarely discovered and reported to law enforcement. In addition, many forms of behavior that may reveal troubling tendencies (bullying or threatening social media posts) may not even be criminal in a technical sense but may serve as precursors of violent behavior.

Cruz, the school shooter in Parkland (Florida), displayed violence, animal abuse, a fascination with guns, and disturbing social media posts.[25] His peers and school officials were aware of his troubling behavior and even notified law enforcement on multiple occasions. He nevertheless passed a background check and was able to purchase an AR-15 military-style rifle because he had no criminal convictions. Many individuals who kill and commit mass shootings have no criminal record and will pass a NICS check.

Judge Richard Gergel of the United States District Court for the District of South Carolina presided over 15 lawsuits filed against the government pursuant to the mass shooting at the Emmanuel Episcopal Church in Charleston. The lawsuits alleged negligence on the part of the FBI in conducting background checks, which resulted in Roof's purchase of the gun used in the mass shooting.

"The record reveals that the FBI's background check system is disturbingly superficial...and obstructed by policies that deny the overworked and overburdened examiners access to the most comprehensive law enforcement federal database,"[26] concluded Judge Gergel about the NICS system.

The FBI denies its examiners access to the National Data Exchange, a database that would have revealed Roof's prior arrest for a drug offense. Knowledge of this arrest would have disqualified the shooter from buying his pistol. The FBI is currently planning to change their procedures and make this database available to their examiners. This change may take two years to roll out.

Ladd Everitt, one of the nation's leading gun violence prevention advocates, has pointed out that the NICS program was designed by the National Rifle Association— yes, the same NRA that for decades has obstructed efforts to regulate firearms and cut gun-related fatalities.[27] Everitt notes that when President Lyndon Johnson signed the Gun Control Act of 1968, he knew that its compromises would undermine the goal of keeping the public safe.

Johnson wrote:

This bill—as big as this bill is—still falls short, because we just could not get the Congress to carry out the requests we made of them. I asked for the national registration of all guns and the licensing of those who carry those guns… If guns are to be kept out of the hands of the criminal, out of the hands of the insane, and out of the hands of the irresponsible, then we just must have licensing. If the criminal with a gun is to be tracked down quickly, then we must have registration in this country. The voices that blocked these safeguards were not the voices of an aroused nation. They were the voices of a powerful lobby, a gun lobby, that has prevailed for the moment in an election year. But the key to effective crime control remains, in my judgment, effective gun control… We must continue to work for the day when Americans can get the full protection that every American citizen is entitled to and deserves—the kind of protection that most civilized nations have long ago adopted.[28]

Americans were outraged after the attempted assassination of President Ronald Reagan in 1981 by John Hinckley, a mentally disturbed man who obtained his gun from a Dallas pawn shop after lying about his state of residence. Everitt points out that, within weeks, legislation was introduced in Congress to create a national waiting period for handgun buyers to allow law enforcement to conduct proper mental health and criminal background checks. This effort did not succeed but in the mid-1980s, Sarah Brady, the wife of Jim Brady (the Reagan adviser who was seriously disabled in the assassination attempt), began her advocacy on behalf of a waiting period. The initial version of the "Brady Bill," introduced in Congress in 1987, called for a seven-day waiting period to conduct a background check.

The NRA opposed the Brady Bill, and Rep. Bill McCollum (R-Florida) introduced an amendment in 1988 to replace it with a point-of-sale instant check that could be initiated by a licensed dealer to screen potential handgun buyers. While intriguing, few states had computerized felony records in 1988, and mental health records were exclusively on paper. The House passed McCollum's amendment and voted the Brady Bill down. However, in 1991, President Reagan, an NRA member, came out in favor of the Brady Bill, saying that the assassination attempt might never have occurred had it been law in 1981.

The NRA and its supporters in Congress persisted in promoting the instant check system, and in 1993, the Brady Handgun Violence Prevention Act was passed requiring the FBI to set up the instant background check system by 1998. The legislation no longer called for a waiting period and gun sales could proceed after three days if the FBI did not find information that would disqualify a gun purchaser. This system, involving no direct contact between law enforcement and the buyer, still exists today. The Florida Scandal illustrates some of the weaknesses of the current system.

The Florida Scandal

Florida, the country's third most populous state, issues the largest number of concealed weapons permits with 1.9 million residents having active permits. A 2018 scandal, however, illustrated the casual and unprofessional manner by which Florida, among other states, administer their permitting and background check systems.[29]

Permits have been issued in Florida by the Department of Agriculture and Consumer Services (DACS)—a strange choice which may now change—and the state Department of Law Enforcement serves as the point of contact for DACS in applications for such permits. In 2017, state investigators discovered that Florida failed to review the results of background checks before issuing permits.

Lisa Wilde, a manager at DACS, was fired following the discovery that she failed to retrieve results of FBI background checks for 13 months, an omission that led to the issuing of gun permits to 300 people who should have been denied. However, she appeared to be singled out unfairly because interviews by investigators with eight employees showed that the screening of applicants was left to overwhelmed mailroom employees who demonstrated little understanding of NICS and why screening was necessary. The permitting process was so poorly understood that the failure to conduct proper background checks went unnoticed by Wilde's supervisor for 13 months. In fact, the supervisor did not even know that Wilde was in charge of the unit.

Other employees said they were swamped by a surge in demand for concealed weapons permits and did not understand the background check system. During the period under review, employees failed to notice that not a single application had been flagged ineligible by the NICS system, even though between 40 and 50 are usually flagged a month. Neither Wilde, her supervisor nor the other employees understood the purpose of the NICS system and its importance. Even Adam Putnam, agriculture commissioner at the time, did not have a full understanding of NICS. The permitting system had broken down previously under Putnam and this was attributed to poor training. Safeguards put in place at the time required random checks of permitting to ensure they were approved properly. The sloppiness of the entire permitting system illustrates Florida's political culture, its antipathy toward any form of gun regulation, and an indifference to public safety.

Solution: A Comprehensive National Licensing System for Gun Owners

The number of mass shooters and other aggressors who have passed existing background checks illustrate the inadequacies of this system. While no system is without flaws, we need a more comprehensive vetting process to get at troubling behavior among those at risk to commit violence. I recommend a comprehensive gun licensing system such as those found in other advanced countries that have a fraction of the gun deaths seen in the US.

Merely expanding the current system of background checks to include private gun sales does not appear to reduce gun violence levels.[30] However, a Johns Hopkins study found that states that adopted licensing as a requirement to purchase a firearm showed a 14 percent reduction in gun homicides in large, urban counties.[31] Licensing more fully involves law enforcement, and the process can allow for time to conduct a more complete investigation into an applicant's background than the dealer-initiated instant background check.

I recommend a licensing system that would consist of the following:

- Law enforcement would conduct an in-person interview with every license applicant.

- A careful review would be conducted of the applicant's criminal, military, and mental health records.

- Personal and work-related references would be interviewed.

- Where applicable, spouses or ex-spouses would be notified of the application and would be afforded the opportunity to inform the authorities of violence, substance abuse, or psychological instability on the part of the applicant.

- Training, including knowledge of the law relating to the use of force, safe handling and storage of firearms, marksmanship, and judgment would be required from an accredited law enforcement agency with written and performance-based tests.

- A waiting period of 15 business days would be established to allow for a "cooling off" period for those who may be in the midst of a personal crisis.

- The license would be renewable every five years.

- Licensing would be retroactive, requiring current gun owners to complete the licensing process.

- Applicants would pay a fee to support the licensing process.

For consideration: a number of countries evaluate the mental and physical fitness of individuals for firearm ownership and impose requirements relating to the storage of their firearms.

3

Regulating the Carrying of Guns

America is not just an outlier in its level of gun ownership. Relative to other advanced countries, it also stands out in terms of the permissiveness of its laws with regard to carrying handguns and in the number of people who have permits or are otherwise authorized to carry guns. Between 8 and 14 million Americans have such permits[32] and a dozen states now allow gun carrying without a permit. The list of these states is growing. At the top of the NRA's wish list is Concealed Carry Reciprocity, which would allow individuals authorized to carry guns in their home state to carry guns in every other state, thereby preventing states that wish to regulate gun carrying more strictly from doing so.[33]

Contrary to popular belief, the widespread carrying of guns is a break from the past; the carrying of concealed firearms was outlawed in about 40 states by the end of the 1800s. Robert Spitzer, a political scientist at the State University of New York at Cortland, notes that the combination of Stand Your Ground laws with escalating civilian gun carrying increases unnecessary violent confrontations and deaths. He adds that we need policies that defuse rather than encourage confrontations.

Spitzer writes:

> *We've learned this lesson before, in our own violent past, when strict regulation of concealed gun carrying was the near-universal and successful response to gun violence. As early as 1686, New Jersey enacted a law against wearing weapons because they induced "great Fear and Quarrels." Massachusetts followed in 1750. In the late 1700s, North Carolina and Virginia passed similar laws. In the 1800s, as interpersonal violence and gun carrying spread, 37 states joined the list. Tennessee's 1821 law fined "each and every person so degrading himself" by carrying weapons in public. Alabama's 1839 law was titled "An Act to Suppress the Evil Practice of Carrying Weapons Secretly." Why must we relearn a lesson we codified centuries ago? How dumb are we?*[34]

With gun carrying, we are no longer talking about gun ownership for the purpose of hunting or target shooting. Gun carrying also extends well beyond the notion of gun ownership for the purpose of the protection of one's family and possessions within the home. As guns are allowed to be brought into more and more settings, there is a growing risk that everyday disputes on the road, in restaurants, on college campuses, and countless other places will escalate from verbal disputes and simple assaults to shootings and homicides. Where states have adopted a version of a Stand Your Ground law (see Chapter 10), individuals may feel more emboldened to use lethal force due to the belief they will receive immunity from prosecution if they use such force in a dispute or in response to a threat.

The carrying of guns raises the possibility that spontaneous disputes and impulsive acts of violence turn lethal, including acts that may have had an entirely different outcome had guns not been available. We are not talking about premeditated acts where one can argue that someone who sets out to kill will find the means to do so regardless of the tools available. We are talking about incidents like road rage, a fight over a parking spot, or a barroom fight in which anger rises and may dissipate quickly. In such incidents, the lethality of the weapons available will make all the difference to the harm produced.

In the late 1980s, states began to pass "shall issue" laws that made it a right to carry a firearm providing an individual did not fall in a prohibited category (e.g., was not a felon, mentally ill, a domestic abuser, or dishonorably discharged from the military). The laws also removed the discretion of law enforcement to deny eligible individuals a permit to carry. The most recent research shows that such carry laws have had an adverse effect on public safety. Professor John Donohue of Stanford University has found that such laws typically increase a state's homicide rates by 13 percent to 15 percent.[35]

The vast majority of states that require a permit to carry mandate a level of training that does not even approximate the knowledge and skills needed to perform in a combat situation. It is no wonder that, even with millions having these permits, cases in which civilians have effectively used a gun to thwart an attacker are quite rare. Consider an FBI study of "active shooter" incidents from 2000 to 2013. In 160 of these cases, an armed civilian intervened to stop the shooting in just one incident.[36]

Experiments with mock school shootings have shown that armed students will often freeze or be shot trying to confront an attacker. Commenting on these studies, Canadian journalist, Jonathan Kay, writes: "When pro-gun activists and politicians make their case, they often regress into adolescent fantasy worlds—where ordinary Joes and Janes are transformed into heroic commandos. In real life, ordinary people faced with a mass-shooter situation are more likely to wet their pants."[37] Recent mass shootings in Parkland and Dallas have shown that even armed police officers and armed right-to-carry activists often will shy away from engaging the shooter.

Joseph Vince, a former agent with the Bureau of Alcohol, Tobacco, Firearms and Explosives for 27 years, is an internationally recognized expert on firearms and gun-related crime. Vince and his collaborators write about the importance of a full vetting of those seeking a license to carry a gun:

> *Since a firearm has immense lethality, the act of carrying one cannot be taken lightly. It should be given to those who have demonstrated good judgment, as well as mastered the necessary skills to handle this awesome responsibility. Legislators need to strengthen the vetting process of persons who are authorized to carry a firearm outside a residence. A simple criminal record check is not sufficient. Preventing criminal or accidental tragedies with firearms begins by allowing only those who have been properly trained initially and ongoing—and are known to be nonviolent law-abiding citizens—to carry in public. Likewise, no one who has anger, mental, or drug/alcohol issues should be permitted to carry a firearm. Certainly, an extensive law enforcement investigation of an applicant's background should be required to detect unsuitable candidates.*[38]

Vince and his associates add that training should include mental preparation, knowledge of the law, and good judgment as well as expertise, skill, and familiarity with firearms. They recommend basic initial training to receive a permit and biannual recertification to maintain the permit. Both training and recertification should consist of decision-making during real-life scenarios, shooting accuracy in stressful situations, and firing range practice.

The Washington-based Violence Policy Center has shown that from May 2007 to August 2018 concealed weapons permit holders around the country have been involved in the killing of 1,259 people, including 31 mass shootings and the murder of 21 police officers.[39] Additional studies in Texas and Florida have documented the sizable number of permit holders who have committed serious crimes.[40] Polls show that large majorities of Americans oppose the repeal of permit requirements and the introduction of guns into many venues, including college campuses, bars, restaurants, hospitals, stadiums, and government buildings.[41] In addition, a number of polls show that the public is worried about gun carrying as more Americans indicate they would feel less, not more, safe if gun carrying in their community increased.[42]

Despite the crimes attributed to concealed weapons permit holders and the desire of the public to restrict gun carrying, the reality is that there are no federal requirements imposed on people who carry guns and most states do not approach the standards recommended by Vince and others. As of August 2018, 12 states required no permit to carry a firearm at all, and the number of "permitless" carry states is growing. Some states requiring permits to carry have no training requirement (e.g. Georgia), and many other states are extremely vague with regard to their requirements. They do not specify the training content, the amount of instruction required, or the score required in written and field proficiency tests.

To illustrate the importance of training and experience in using firearms when threatened, retired Army Sergeant Rafael Noboa y Rivera, who led a combat team in Iraq, says that soldiers generally only function effectively following exposure to fire on multiple occasions. Unlike gunplay as depicted in the movies, Rivera says:

> When I heard gunfire [in Iraq], I didn't immediately pick up my rifle and react. I first tried to ascertain where the shooting was coming from, where I was in relation to the gunfire and how far away it was. I think most untrained people are either going to freeze up, or just whip out their gun and start firing in that circumstance.[43]

Similarly, David Chipman, a former agent with the ATF who spent several years on the agency's SWAT team, says, "Training for a potentially deadly encounter meant, at a minimum, qualifying four times a year throughout my 25-year career. And this wasn't just shooting paper—it meant doing extensive tactical exercises. And when I was on the SWAT team we had to undergo monthly tactical training."

Tactical officers receive training in "judgmental shooting," which includes knowing when it is wise to hold their fire and "blue-on-blue awareness," which reinforces the importance of considering whether other officers are present.[44]

Research and police records show that even trained police officers miss their targets more often than they hit them during stressful combat situations. Greg Morrison, a former police officer and firearms instructor, says there is some agreement among practitioners and researchers that in real-life crime situations, officers hit the mark once in every six shots—a 17 percent proficiency level in combat situations. Records of firearm discharges indicate that the New York City Police Department (NYPD) has a 34 percent hit ratio (proficiency level); however, this rate falls to 18 percent when the target is shooting at officers.[45]

We would logically expect the average civilian gun owner to do much worse. Civilian owners receive little or no marksmanship training and, unlike law enforcement, they are not required to undergo continued training. Ordinarily, civilian gun owners do not receive training in judgment and are less knowledgeable about the law—that is, those circumstances in which lethal force is permissible.

Judgment refers to an armed person's ability to make appropriate "shoot/don't shoot" decisions in a stressful situation. The goal is to minimize errors—in other words, shooting when not necessary and failing to shoot when one's life is in danger. Many police departments use firearms training simulators that expose officers to a number of high-risk scenarios for training purposes. The aim is to achieve the best judgment possible during threatening situations. The lack of training of gun carriers in most states is reflected in the many examples of catastrophic errors by individuals who are frightened and have guns in their possession or nearby. Humans will always misperceive threats; however, the presence of guns and a lack of restraint in using them make fatal errors far more likely.

Consider some of the following cases:

- A 21-year-old Iowa woman was killed after she, along with her younger sister, tried to surprise her fiancé by hiding in a closet in his home. He heard a noise and saw the closet door open. When the girls jumped out of the closet, he fired and killed his fiancé with a handgun he kept for protection.

- A seven-year-old boy was in critical condition after his grandmother mistook him for an intruder and shot him. She and her twin grandsons were sleeping after their father went to work. When she heard the bedroom door open, she assumed it was an intruder, grabbed the loaded revolver she kept by her bed and fired one shot toward the door. As it turned out, she shot her grandson in the upper body.

- A 20-year-old mother was watching television in her parents' home when she heard noises outside the bedroom wall. She had heard stories of recent burglaries in the neighborhood. Though she had no weapons training, she picked up a semiautomatic pistol. She clumsily fired a number of shots and hit her eight-month-old son in the head. He died several hours later.

Joseph Vince and his colleagues say that the average violent attack is over in three seconds. This is how they describe a typical attack:

They are "blitz" attacks, designed to blindside and overwhelm us. We must be able to comprehend what's happening, orient ourselves to that attack, draw, and begin fighting back within that three-second window, or else there's a very good chance we'll be defeated before we have a chance to even draw our weapons. The problem is, our bodies don't only choose between Fight and Flight, but instead between Fight, Flight, and Freeze. And without specific training, many (if not most) of us are prone to freezing for three or more seconds when confronted with a sudden, psychologically and physically overwhelming attack. We need training that will allow us to avoid violence whenever possible, but overcome, defeat, and survive violence when we can't avoid it.[46]

Kentucky firearms instructor Rick Strohmeier adds, " I have people who come to my class who basically couldn't hit the broad side of a barn… It takes 2,500 repetitions to pick up a pistol correctly."[47]

Just half of all states require the firing of a weapon as part of the permitting process. As an illustration of the education/training, consider Florida, the state that pioneered the modern permissive "shall issue" laws and that has more concealed weapons permit holders than any other—close to two million by the end of 2018.[48] Permit holders in Florida have a criminal record check, must complete a gun safety course (with some exceptions), submit an application, and get fingerprinted.

Florida Statutes Chapter 790.06 does not spell out the contents of the course; it merely indicates the qualifications the instructors must possess (e.g. certification by the NRA or the Department of Florida Fish and Wildlife) or the organizations that may offer the course. It does not specify whether the course needs to include instruction on the safe handling of firearms, when it is appropriate to use lethal force against another person, what constitutes good judgment (when to shoot/not to shoot), how to hold and load a gun, and the extent to which the course should teach marksmanship.

The three-hour course taken by this writer involved classroom instruction (although an insurance product was pitched for about 20 minutes), and the rest of the course involved waiting for and ultimately taking five shots with a handgun at a firing range.

During the class, the instructor handed out literature offering one-on-one courses in shooting fundamentals, handling skills, and maintenance/cleaning of guns, implying that the concealed weapons course did not cover gun handling or shooting fundamentals. When I had inquired about the course over the phone, I was told that they had never failed anyone. The course contents were very basic, covering the use of force, gun safety fundamentals, and the settings into which the applicant can bring a gun. There was no shooting accuracy requirement to complete the course. Nor was there any test of shooting accuracy, gun handling, information retention, or training on judgment (when to shoot and when not to shoot), which involves simulators or real-world exercises. Everyone passes regardless of what they have learned and how they do on the firing range.

An especially troubling aspect of firearms training in Florida, as well as in most states, is that training is provided by private businesses rather than law enforcement. Operators have an enormous financial interest in passing everyone as these will be future customers for the gun store or firing range. In other countries, law enforcement is responsible for these courses, has more rigorous standards, and is not afraid to fail people if they do not demonstrate a reasonable level of competency.

Recommendations:

- National standards should exist with regard to the training requirements for carrying firearms. This is especially the case given the proposal, referred to as Concealed Carry Reciprocity, that would allow individuals to seamlessly cross state lines and carry in all states rather than simply the one in which a license was issued or in states with which a state has a reciprocal agreement.

- Until national standards are enacted, Concealed Carry Reciprocity should be vigorously resisted because it would lower the standard nationally, undermine states that are making serious efforts to regulate the carrying of guns, and as research shows would very likely lead to an increase in gun homicides.

- In addition to the vetting required by licensing owners (Chapter 2), carry permit applicants should receive enhanced training in the law (when it is permissible to use lethal force) and real-life training in the use of firearms in combat situations. Training should be ongoing rather than simply to qualify for a license.

- In order to avoid conflicts of interest, training should be conducted by law enforcement and not by a private business.

- Carrying without a permit should not exist anywhere in the United States. This is what gun rights advocates refer to as Constitutional Carry; however, nowhere does the US Constitution grant the right of individuals to carry guns for their own protection.

The late US Supreme Court Justice, Antonin Scalia, an avid hunter, wrote in *District of Columbia v. Heller* that the Second Amendment to the Constitution does not guarantee a right to carry firearms. He wrote:

Like most rights, the Second Amendment right is not unlimited. It is not a right to keep and carry any weapon whatsoever in any manner whatsoever and for whatever purpose: For example, concealed weapons prohibitions have been upheld under the Amendment or state analogues.[49]

4

Keeping Guns from Dangerous Individuals

Currently, federal law prohibits the sale of firearms to individuals who:

- Have been convicted of, or are under indictment for, a crime punishable by a prison term of over one year.

- Are fugitives from justice.

- Are unlawful users of or addicted to a controlled substance.

- Are under the minimum age. (For sales by licensed dealers, the purchaser of a handgun must be 21, and for a long gun, the buyer must be 18 years of age. Unlicensed persons may sell long guns to persons of any age and are prohibited from selling a handgun or handgun ammunition to persons they have reasonable cause to believe are under 18 years of age, with the exception of certain temporary transfers for specified activities, like employment.)

- Have been adjudicated as a mental defective or committed to a psychiatric institution.

- Are not lawfully in the USA or were admitted under a nonimmigrant visa.

- Were dishonorably discharged from the military.

- Have renounced their US citizenship.

- Are subject to a court order restraining them from harassing, stalking, or threatening an intimate partner or child.

- Have been convicted of a misdemeanor domestic violence offense.

While there has been much emphasis on the role of mental illness in gun violence, federal law already prohibits individuals who are "mentally defective" from buying guns. This prohibition has been difficult to implement due to inconsistent reporting to the FBI of mental health information by the states and, regardless, mental illness *per se* is a questionable predictor of violence. Just a small fraction of violent acts are committed by the mentally ill, and most of these individuals are not a threat to the public.[50]

More troubling are domestic abusers (including those in dating relationships), stalkers, individuals with impulsive and explosive anger issues, those communicating serious threats of violence, and substance abusers, especially those with a history of violence or mental illness. Domestic violence affects millions of people, and 4.5 million American women have had an intimate partner threaten them or a loved one with a gun. Nearly one million women alive today have been shot or shot at by an intimate partner.[51] Many mass shootings, too, have a connection to domestic violence.

Jeffrey Swanson of Duke University and his associates have found that about 22 million Americans (about 9 percent of the population) have impulsive anger issues (explosive, uncontrollable rage) and easy access to guns.[52] Close to four million of these angry gun owners routinely carry their guns in public and they are typically young or middle-aged men. Age is usually related to the risk of violence. Many school shooters and a significant percentage of violent felons are under the age of 21.[53]

Aside from prohibiting at-risk individuals from purchasing guns, a mechanism is required to remove guns from individuals deemed to be dangerous once they have acquired guns. Individuals may become mentally ill, issue threats, or exhibit disturbing behavior that comes to the attention of family members, peers, or law enforcement personnel. A growing number of states have been introducing Extreme Risk Protection Orders (also known as "red flag" laws) that allow law enforcement and, in some cases, family members or roommates to petition a court to remove guns from individuals deemed to be dangerous to themselves or others.

An FBI study of active shooter situations between 2000 and 2013 found that the average active shooter displayed four to five concerning and observable behaviors, including signs of mental illness, problematic relationships, or an intention to commit violence.[54] However, those witnessing danger signs did not notify authorities or authorities lacked the legal tools to intervene and seize the eventual shooter's weapons.

Prior to these recently enacted red flag laws, Connecticut and Indiana passed laws allowing law enforcement officers or other individuals to obtain court orders that would remove firearms from dangerous people.[55] A 2016 study showed that in Connecticut, one suicide was prevented for every 10-

20 guns seized under the law. Indiana's law was associated with 7.5 percent fewer suicides in the state following its passage in 2005.

In May 2014, a young man shot 10 people in Isla Vista, California. He also hit seven people with his car and stabbed three more before committing suicide. Prior to this incident, his parents were so concerned about his behavior that they contacted his therapist, who informed police that he was likely to harm himself or others. The police interviewed him but stated that they did not have the legal authority to remove the shooter's guns or take him into custody. Following the mass murder, several states, including California, passed expanded versions of the laws in Connecticut and Indiana. In some states, these laws allow family members, as well as law enforcement, to petition a court to keep guns away from a dangerous person in the midst of a crisis.

States provide guidance to courts assessing whether a person is at an elevated risk of violence. For example, in California, the court must consider the following evidence:[56]

- Threats or acts of violence, either self-directed or towards another, within the previous six months.

- A violation of a domestic violence emergency protective order that is in effect when the court is considering the petition.

- A violation of an unexpired domestic violence protective order within the past six months.

- Any criminal conviction prohibiting the purchase and possession of firearms.

- A pattern of violent acts or threats within the previous year.

California courts may also consider other evidence that is indicative of an increased risk for violence, such as the reckless use of a firearm, threats or use of physical force, prior felony arrests, violations of domestic violence protective orders, criminal offenses within the past six months involving controlled substances or alcohol, evidence of ongoing chemical abuse, and recent acquisition of firearms and ammunition.

In addition to red flag laws, a small number of states (e.g. Massachusetts, New York) require a license to possess firearms. These states have a procedure to revoke a person's firearm license if the individual poses a danger to themselves or others.

Recommendations:

I recommend adding that anyone should be prohibited by federal law (see the list above) from purchasing or *possessing* firearms if they meet any of the following criteria:

- Have been convicted of a violent misdemeanor.

- Have been convicted of two or more drug or alcohol-related offenses (including driving offenses) within a five-year period.

- Violated a restraining order issued due to a threat of violence.

- Harassed, stalked, or threatened a dating partner or former partner.

- Have been convicted of misdemeanor stalking.

- Are subject to a temporary restraining order. (All states should establish a mechanism whereby family members or law enforcement can petition a court to temporarily remove firearms from a family member if they believe there is a substantial likelihood that the person is a significant danger to himself or others.)

- Have recently experienced a short-term involuntary hospitalization. (They should be subject to a temporary ban on gun purchases or possession.)

In addition, voluntary outpatient commitments should disqualify individuals temporarily from purchasing or possessing firearms if there is a court finding of substantial likelihood of future danger to self or others or an equivalent finding. The age of 21 should be established as the minimum age for the purchase or possession of a firearm.

Where applicable, firearm license applications (see Chapter 2) should require a signature or notification of current and former spouses/cohabiting partners. This step will help identify individuals who are prone to violence that may have gone unreported. The states should be incentivized to provide complete reporting of all people who fall in a prohibited class due to criminal offenses or mental illness. Alternatively, federal resources should be utilized to gather state criminal and mental health data. Publicly funded educational institutions and the military should be obligated to report people identified as violent or suicidal to a law enforcement agency or licensing body.

5

Safe Storage to Prevent Unauthorized Access to Guns

Each year, approximately 1,300 children die in America from a gunshot wound and close to five million children live in homes where at least one gun is loaded and unlocked. In about two out of three school shootings, the young perpetrator obtained his guns from his home or from that of a relative.[57] Among the most recent cases was the murder of 10 people and wounding of another 13 at a high school in Santa Fe, Texas. In addition, inadequate gun storage contributes to the theft of 300,000 guns each year.

Mark Shuster and his colleagues at the UCLA School of Medicine analyzed data from the National Health Interview Survey and found that 43 percent of American homes with children and firearms had at least one firearm that was not locked in a container and not locked with a trigger lock or other locking mechanism.[58] A more recent national survey by Johns Hopkins Bloomberg School of Public Health found that more than half of all gun owners failed to store all their guns safely. Children under 18 were present in a third of these homes.[59]

Many children under 10 years of age—three-quarters according to one study—know the location of their parents' firearms and many admit to handling the weapons.[60] In many cases, the parents were not aware that their children knew the storage location of household guns nor that their children had handled a household gun. Many young children are strong enough to pull the trigger on a firearm.

In some countries, the safe storage of firearms—storing firearms unloaded and/or in a locked container—is a condition of gun ownership. In the US, there is an absence of national requirements relating to gun storage, and the majority of states have adopted laws enabling armed self-defense both in the home and in public places. Gun storage practices are weakening as more people are now keeping guns for self-defense, and many have bought into the NRA narrative that guns in the home make us safer. Safe storage is viewed by armed self-defense advocates as an impediment to those desiring quick access to a loaded weapon. However, there are many solutions that allow for both safe storage and rapid deployment of a gun. Also, safe storage ordinances, such as one in San Francisco, have been upheld by the lower courts, which have ruled that present-day locking devices can be opened fast enough to allow for effective self-defense.[61]

The US General Accounting Office has estimated that close to a third of accidental deaths by firearms can be prevented by the addition of childproof safety locks and loaded chamber indicators that provide a visual and tactile (for darkness) indication that there is a round in the firearm's chamber.[62] Studies of child access prevention laws, which require owners to store their guns so that children and teens cannot access them without supervision, have found that these laws prevent a significant number of accidental shootings of children and adolescent suicides and that these laws are among the most effective measures in preventing gun-related injuries and fatalities.[63]

Currently, about a dozen states have some kind of mandatory storage rules, but only Massachusetts has a law requiring that all firearms be secured without exemptions. Research shows that more children are killed with firearms where weaker state laws exist.[64]

Gun safety training for adults, teens, and children has been suggested as a way of reducing accidental shootings. However, numerous surveys and experiments show that the majority of programs have not been successful in improving storage practices, the safe handling of guns by teens, or in getting children who come across guns to avoid handling them.

In one study, a police officer instructed a group of children to leave an area and inform an adult if they came across a gun. The message was clear that they should avoid touching guns. Through the use of hidden cameras, ABC's *20/20* program documented the fact that children, while verbalizing the instructions they received, consistently handled real unloaded guns, pointed them at other children or themselves, and even pulled the trigger. Parents were horrified to see their children disobeying what they had been taught minutes earlier and the potential consequences should their children encounter loaded guns. The lesson appears to be that gun safety training should be a minor part of gun accident prevention for children and youth. In initiatives involving children, too much of an onus is placed on the children, who are not mature enough to consider the consequences of their actions, and it is evident that guns need to be secured and inaccessible to them.

The evidence is similar with regard to teens. The American Academy of Pediatrics Committee on Adolescence has concluded that due to their inherent sense of invincibility, curiosity, immaturity, and impulsiveness, "…educational efforts aimed at teaching teenagers to use guns safely are not likely to be successful in preventing firearm death and injury. No published research confirms effectiveness of gun safety training for adolescents."[65]

Americans strongly support laws requiring the safe storage of firearms. A national survey conducted in January 2013 found that two-thirds of Americans, including almost half of those owning guns, support laws requiring gun owners to lock up any guns in the home when not in use in order to prevent handling by children or teenagers without adult supervision.[66]

Unlike many other advanced countries, the US has no national laws relating to how firearms should be stored and lacks national standards that would ensure that locking devices and gun safes do not fail. Massachusetts is the only state that requires owners to store all firearms with a lock in place.[67] That state has a much lower gun suicide rate among youth than the US as a whole, and this may be due, at least in part, to the infrequent use of guns in suicide attempts.[68] Three states require storing guns with a locking device where an individual ineligible to possess a firearm resides in the same household. Fourteen states and the District of Columbia hold individuals who store firearms negligently criminally liable when minors can or do gain access to them.

Seattle shows that cities can act when states and the federal government fail to do so. Following the release of a study showing that nearly two in three gun-owning households in the state of Washington do not store their firearms safely, the city enacted an ordinance requiring the safe storage of firearms within city limits unless the gun was being carried by the owner or authorized user.[69] The ordinance also increased civil penalties and legal responsibility for failing to report unsecured firearms that have been lost, stolen, or improperly used by an unauthorized user.

The purpose of the legislation has been to encourage responsible behavior rather than to punish residents. The concern was that many improperly secured weapons were being used by young people in suicides or involved in accidental shootings. Under the ordinance, a gun owner could face fines of up to $500 for failure to store a gun in a locked container. The fine would increase to $1,000 if a minor or prohibited person was in possession of an unsecured weapon and up to $10,000 if a minor or prohibited person used an unsecured firearm to cause injury, death, or to commit a crime.

A recent report from the Rand Corporation shows that child-access prevention or safe storage laws may be among the most effective forms of gun regulation.[70] According to Rand, available evidence supports the conclusion that safe storage laws reduce self-inflicted fatal or nonfatal firearm injuries among youth and unintentional firearm injuries and deaths among children. Also, there is some evidence that these laws may reduce unintentional firearm injuries among adults.

Initiatives to secure guns do not necessarily involve legislation, which can be challenging due to the political clout of the gun lobby and its supporters. One example of a voluntary program is Lock it Up, a program developed by Barbara Markley and the Gun Safety Committee of the Broward County (Florida) League of Women Voters.[71] The program aims to encourage gun owners to lock up their guns to protect children from guns and to reduce suicide. It recognizes that over 50 percent of teens who commit suicide with a gun obtain the gun at home.

The program has two main elements: Raising public awareness and providing free access to one method of securing firearms. For public awareness, a brochure is being produced with a photo of a child reaching for a gun and statistics about the dangers of unsecured guns around children. The brochure is being disseminated throughout the county, including parks, government buildings, pediatrician and child psychologist offices, and at large public events. The second component of the program involves offering people a means of securing their weapons at no cost to them. Markley and her colleagues learned that the VA has a large supply of trigger locks due to veterans' elevated risk of suicide. They obtained a free supply, and their goal is to place these brochures and free trigger locks in every pediatrician's office in Broward County. They also plan to present public forums with expert panels on depression, suicide, and gun safety.

This is the type of program that is accessible to all, including gun-owning households in low-income neighborhoods. Who can possibly oppose a program that is voluntary, does not increase public expenditures, educates people about gun safety, and can be implemented promptly as it requires no legislation to be passed? This is the type of grassroots innovative program that can change attitudes relating to gun safety and be embraced by gun owners and gun safety advocates alike.

Recommendations:

- National standards should be established for firearm locking devices to ensure that they are both effective and allow for rapid deployment of weapons, bearing in mind the right of Americans to possess firearms for self-defense in the home.

- Laws regarding the safe storage of firearms and the prevention of access by minors and unauthorized persons ought to be considered by the federal government.

- State laws, where they exist, should be strengthened to ensure that gun owners are liable for harm resulting from their failure to store guns safely and out of reach of minors.

- The federal government should launch a public education campaign to inform Americans about the extent of gun deaths and the benefits of safe storage, especially around children and teens.

- As part of the qualifications for gun ownership, owners should be educated about their responsibilities with regard to safe storage and informed about the most effective storage options.

- Counties and municipalities, non-profit organizations, and gun dealers should consider offering education regarding the securing of weapons and locking devices at little or no cost to owners. Innovative voluntary and volunteer-based programs, such as the Lock It Up program in Broward County, should be pursued.

- Physician "gag laws" that aim to keep doctors from asking about and providing advice relating to guns in the home should be opposed and repealed.

Part II

Regulating Firearms

6

Restricting or Banning
Weapons of War

Unless one has lived in a cave over the last 20 years or so, it has become apparent that mass shootings are an increasing concern in the US. The deadliest massacres have almost always involved the use of weapons like the AR-15 and its relatives in Las Vegas (with the aid of bump stocks), at the Orlando Pulse nightclub, the church shooting in Sutherland Springs (Texas), the Aurora (Colorado) Century Theater, and school massacres in Newtown (Connecticut) and Parkland. One analysis found that an average of eight more people are shot where these weapons or high-capacity magazines (HCM) are used, illustrating the emptiness of the slogan: "Guns don't kill, people do."[72] In addition, an increasing number of other serious violent crimes, including the murder of police officers, are being committed with assault-style weapons (AW).[73]

An analysis conducted for my book, *Confronting Gun Violence in America,* shows that the number of public mass killings by firearms more than doubled from the 1980s to the 1990s and 2000s.[74] Between 2010 and 2015, the annual number of incidents again increased sharply, at more than four times the frequency observed in the 1980s. More than half of the 30 deadliest mass shootings since 1949 have occurred since 2007. The average number of deaths per year resulting from mass public shootings also has increased and, since 2010, was almost four times that of the 1980s. It is worth noting that the acceleration in the number of large-scale mass shootings occurred following the expiration of the national assault weapons ban in 2004.

The increasing annual number of fatalities is especially noteworthy because great strides have been made in the management of bullet wounds over the last 15 years due to lessons learned on the battlefields of Afghanistan. Survival rates also have increased due to the spread of hospital trauma centers, increased use of helicopters to transport patients, and better training of first responders. Despite higher survival rates, we have seen a rising death toll from mass shootings when we would have expected the opposite. Increasing injuries and deaths reflect, at least in part, the greater lethality of weapons and a higher proportion of victims who suffer multiple bullet wounds. We know that there has been a growing number of military-style weapons in the civilian market after the gun industry introduced them in the 1980s to cater to a core clientele with conventional firearms that was predominantly white, male, and rural.

Dr. Andrew Peitzman, chief of general surgery at the University of Pittsburgh Medical Center, notes that the typical shooting victim today has at least three bullet wounds.[75] Data from the Cook County (Illinois) Medical Examiner's Office found that the average person killed with a firearm in August 2016 was struck by 4.25 rounds, nearly twice the number of rounds as those mortally wounded by a gun in 1992, a peak year for homicide. Semiautomatic pistols fed by magazines holding 10 or more rounds are said to be responsible in many cases for multiple gunshot wounds experienced by victims, according to ATF data.[76]

This is what Dr. Jeremy Cannon of the University of Pennsylvania's Perelman School of Medicine says about the damage produced by high-velocity bullets shot with an AR-15 assault-type weapon: "The tissue destruction is almost unimaginable. Bones are exploded, soft tissue is absolutely destroyed. The injuries to the chest or abdomen— it's like a bomb went off."[77] He's not alone. Surgeons speak of exit wounds that are as long as a foot due to the speed and tumbling of the bullets.

Following the Parkland high school shooting, Heather Sher, a radiologist working in a nearby trauma center, wrote about the injuries delivered by a military-style weapon:

> One of the trauma surgeons opened a young victim in the operating room, and found only shreds of the organ that had been hit by a bullet from an AR-15, a semiautomatic rifle that delivers a devastatingly lethal, high-velocity bullet to the victim. Nothing was left to repair—and utterly, devastatingly, nothing could be done to fix the problem. The injury was fatal.[78]

The Assault Weapons Ban of 1994

The federal ban, in force between 1994 and 2004, prohibited the manufacture, transfer, and possession of semiautomatic firearms designated assault weapons. The weapons subject to the ban were characterized by features suited to military and criminal applications rather than sport shooting or self-defense. More than 100 firearm models, including certain pistols and shotguns, were covered. The ban also covered HCMs holding more than 10 rounds of ammunition, thereby applying to many non-banned weapons that could be equipped with these magazines. At the time the ban took effect, it was estimated that 1.5 million AWs were privately-owned in the US along with about 25 million HCMs. Millions more of the HCMs manufactured before the ban were exempted and imported into the country during the ban.

The ban yielded mixed results with regard to its effect on violent crime. While there was no discernible reduction in gun crime or gun homicide in six major cities—Baltimore, Boston, Miami, St. Louis, Anchorage, and Milwaukee—the share of gun crimes committed with weapons covered by the ban declined by between 17 percent and 72 percent.[79] Nationally, traces of guns used in crimes were 70 percent less likely to involve AWs. Louis Klarevas, author of *Rampage Nation*, found that gun massacres, defined as incidents involving six or more fatalities, were nearly cut in half during the ban in comparison with the previous 10-year period.[8] In the decade following the ban's expiration, fatalities again increased dramatically, more than tripling.

The reduction in crime involving assault weapons was, in part, limited by the substitution of military-style firearms that technically did not qualify as AWs. Also, grandfathering provisions of the AWs ban, which allowed weapons and HCMs already manufactured to continue to be sold, undercut its effectiveness. Approximately 25 million of these magazines remained in the country, and millions more were available for import from other countries. In fact, manufacturers took advantage of the grandfathering provisions by boosting production of designated AWs in the months leading up to the ban, creating a large stockpile of these items. By contrast, in Australia's well-known and successful ban, pre-ban weapons were bought back rather than exempted from the ban.

The manner in which weapons covered by the ban were defined also limited its effectiveness. The federal ban and current state laws define assault weapons by their features, some of which are irrelevant to the harm the weapon can produce. Under the 1994 ban, an assault weapon included semiautomatic rifles capable of accepting detachable magazines and possessing two or more of the following features:

- Folding stocks for concealment and portability

- Pistol grips protruding conspicuously beneath the action of the weapon

- Bayonet mount

- Grenade launcher

- Flash suppressor or threaded barrel designed to accommodate a flash suppressor

Definitions based on these features created a loophole by allowing manufacturers to circumvent the law simply by making minor modifications to a weapon. For example, removing flash suppressors and bayonet mounts makes a weapon no less lethal but can get around a features-based definition.

Overall, the 1994 ban showed some promise but the potential effectiveness was reduced by the grandfathering provisions and the features-based definition of "assault-style" weapons. The ban's exemption of millions of AWs and HCMs manufactured before the ban also meant that the impact of the law would not be fully realized since those weapons kept pouring into the market.

The Australian Ban

In April 1996, a 28-year-old man with significant intellectual disabilities went on a killing spree in Port Arthur, Tasmania, a former penal colony and popular tourist destination south of Melbourne, Australia. A total of 35 people were killed, and 23 people were wounded. The shooter was armed with semiautomatic rifles that were legally available in Tasmania but banned in other states.

Australia is a large country with a frontier history and an established gun culture. Prior to the massacre, the gun lobby and some sympathetic legislators frustrated efforts to develop more restrictive gun laws that would apply across the country. The massacre and the reaction of Prime Minister John Howard, just six weeks in office, represented a turning point. Despite the fact that he headed a conservative party that was a natural ally of the gun lobby and drew much of its support from rural regions with many gun owners, Mr. Howard quickly came to the conclusion that strong national legislation was necessary, including a ban on automatic and semiautomatic long guns.

When some states resisted his proposed reforms, he threatened to hold a national referendum to alter the Australian Constitution and give the federal government power over gun policy. Public opinion was on his side, although opposition to major gun reforms was very vocal and threatening. As a result of the national government's leadership, Australia's federal and state governments agreed to harmonize firearm laws across the country in a series of agreements.

The most comprehensive law, the National Firearms Agreement (NFA) of 1996, included a ban on the sale, importation, or possession of primarily automatic and semiautomatic long arms.[81] A buyback scheme was implemented in order to compensate owners for the forfeiture of firearms that were now banned. The NFA also called for a uniform licensing and registration system in all eight states and territories of Australia, a 28-day waiting period, safety training for all first-time licensees, and a uniform standard for the security and storage of firearms.

Estimates indicate that approximately one million firearms—up to a third of the national inventory of privately held guns—were bought back or surrendered voluntarily between 1996 and 2003. The majority of studies and analyses indicate that the NFA provided significant public safety benefits. For example, Philip Alpers of the University of Sydney's School of Public Health, noted that 100 people died in 11 mass shootings in the decade leading up to Australia's legislative reforms in 1996. Since these reforms were announced and as of January 2013, he noted that there have been no mass murders by firearm in Australia.[82] In 2014, there was one family murder-suicide by firearm, 18 years after the new laws were introduced.

Simon Chapman and his colleagues at the University of Sydney compared firearm-related homicides, suicides, and unintentional deaths before and after the legislative reforms and observed that firearm deaths declined from 628 per year from 1979 to 1996 (prior to the announcement of the new gun laws) to 333 per year following the announcement (1997–2003).[83] Firearm suicides declined from 492 per year before the reforms were announced to 247 per year following the introduction of the new laws. Suicides by other methods also declined, indicating that reducing the availability of firearms did not lead to a compensating increase in suicides by other means. Firearm homicides declined from 93 per year prior to the reforms to 56 per year after the reforms. There was no compensating increase in homicides by means other than a firearm.

Three Proposed Solutions for the US

Option #1:

All banned firearms would be bought back from their owners at a fair market price and destroyed. There would be no grandfather provision that would allow the sale or possession of existing weapons subject to the ban. The buyback would be paid for through a special tax on guns and ammunition.

As far as a definition of assault-style weapons subject to the ban, here is a suggestion that would make it difficult for a manufacturer to modify weapons in a cosmetic way and circumvent the ban:

> *An assault weapon is a semiautomatic rifle with a modular design that can accommodate any one of the following features:*
>
> - *Folding or bump stock*
>
> - *External magazine holding 10 or more rounds of ammunition*
>
> - *Laser or other aiming devices*
>
> - *Any other feature that increases, from its basic configuration, the muzzle velocity, rate of fire, accuracy, range, or lethality of the firearm.*

Pistols that can receive external magazines of more than 10 rounds also would be banned, as would all such magazines or other ammunition feeding devices.

Option #2:

Assault weapons and pistols capable of receiving external, high-capacity magazines would be regulated in the same manner as fully automatic firearms (machine guns), short-barreled rifles and shotguns, silencers, various explosive devices, and certain firearms with bores of over half an inch.

The National Firearms Act (NFA), enacted in 1934, specifies that weapons regulated under the NFA must be registered, and individuals wishing to buy these weapons must undergo a background check, including photographing and fingerprinting, pay a tax, and be subject to severe penalties for noncompliance.[84] Waiting periods to obtain an NFA weapon are extensive. Dealers selling such weapons must have special licenses. As of April 2017, there were about 630,000 registered machine guns in the US, and very few have been used in crimes.[85] It is worth noting that the manufacture and importation of fully automatic weapons in the US for civilian use has been banned since 1986.

I do not recommend this option. There are 10-15 million semiautomatic AWs in civilian hands in the US and a large number of pistols that can receive high-capacity magazines (HCMs). Grandfathering an amendment to the NFA (exempting existing owners from the new requirements) would leave an enormous inventory of these weapons in the hands of owners who would be exempted from the tougher screening required under the Act. This would not serve public safety. Going forward, without a ban on these weapons, the inventory would continue to grow as these weapons would be more tightly controlled but maintain their legal status.

If current owners of AWs and pistols designed for combat have to go through the same vetting procedures as people buying machine guns, they would have to surrender their weapons or stop using them until all the steps required under the NFA were completed. There may well be a compliance problem, due to the steps and fees required. The vetting of owners would be more thorough under my licensing proposal than the background checks currently done for NFA weapons. But at the end of the day, the large inventory of AWs would not be removed from society and a fair number might remain in the hands of those who are noncompliant.

If there is no ban going forward, I do not anticipate that regulation of AR-15s and its relatives through the NFA would be as successful as in the case of machine guns because no attempt would be made to reduce the number of these weapons other than to impose a process that would be an annoyance to buyers. Individuals owning AR-15s and the like are far more numerous than machine gun owners, and they also may fall into a more high-risk group. In fact, a survey in California found that most AWs are owned by a subgroup of super owners—that is, individuals who own at least 10 guns.[86]

Option #3:

This option would be a hybrid solution. Existing AWs would be regulated under the NFA as in Option #2. Going forward, there would be a complete ban on semiautomatic rifles that could receive an external magazine. Internal, built-in magazines would be limited to 10 rounds so one could still own an AR-15 or one of its relatives but its ability to produce great carnage would be limited by the need to stop and reload more often.

I have two concerns with this option. Millions of existing AWs that can receive HCMs would remain in circulation providing the owners received enhanced screening (relative to the current instant background checks) and providing the guns were registered. People not yet owning an AW could still obtain one on the private market from existing owners, even if the capacity for large-scale carnage would be diminished by the need to frequently reload the weapons. Politically, I suspect opposition to reducing the capacity of these weapons to fire many rounds without reloading may be comparable to the opposition to an outright ban.

Recommendations:

I favor a full ban because the massacres we are seeing cannot continue without lasting damage to our sense of security, to our communities, and even to the economy, as people will increasingly avoid public spaces and venues they believe will place them at risk of being caught in the middle of a mass shooting. Option #2 is not designed to reduce the inventory of these weapons at all, and it would take too long to reduce this inventory under Option #3. Many mass shooters are suicidal and would not be deterred by the registration, penalties, and other aspects of regulation under the NFA. Weapons of war should not be in the hands of civilians, especially when far too many civilians have misused them with catastrophic consequences.

7

Using Technology to Enhance Gun Safety

Another way of preventing unauthorized access to guns by children and youth, as well as deterring gun thefts, is through the use of personalizing technologies that lock a gun unless it is activated by the owner or other authorized person. In addition, guns incorporating personalizing technologies can protect police officers who have had their firearm taken by an aggressor.

According to the National Physicians Alliance, almost 95,000 people were injured in the US from unintentional shootings from 2005 to 2010 and nearly half of the victims of these shootings were under 25 years of age.[87] Accidental shootings include scenarios like these:

- A young man, who is joking around with friends, pulls the ammunition magazine out of a gun. Then, believing it is unloaded, he holds it to his head and fires. Tragically, the young man dies, unaware the gun could be loaded and ready to fire even without the detachable magazine. Firearms can be equipped with a "magazine disconnect mechanism" that prevents them from discharging when the magazine is not attached. They can also be equipped with a "chamber loading indicator" that lets the user know when the gun is loaded and ready to fire.

- A child finds a gun in a night table drawer, thinks it is a toy, and pulls the trigger, killing his sister. A number of safety devices can prevent such an accident. The gun may have a trigger lock engaged when not used by its owner. It may also possess one of a number of personalizing features that would allow only the lawful owner to fire the gun.

- A woman accidentally drops a gun. The gun discharges, wounding her husband. Poorly constructed guns can fire without the trigger being pulled. This situation is characteristic of cheap, low-quality, or "junk guns" that may be built with inferior materials and are aimed at a less affluent market.

Currently, no federal agency oversees the design of firearms. The Consumer Product Safety Commission has been explicitly prohibited by Congress from regulating firearms as it does every other major consumer product, including those associated with far fewer injuries and deaths.[88] The quality and risk posed by hair dryers, involved in 20 injuries in 20 years, are regulated as are toys and mattresses. With the exception of a small number of states that impose their own standards, firearm manufacturers are not required to consider the safety of the products they make. Designing for product safety can include ensuring that guns have certain safety features and undergo tests to ensure they do not fire when dropped or malfunction in other ways.

Personalizing guns represents a new way of ensuring that unauthorized users cannot fire them, including children and people stealing guns. In addition to saving lives, personalizing weapons also removes the incentive to steal guns. Some of the deaths and injuries caused by stolen guns also can be prevented. For instance, Stephen Teret and Adam Mernit of Johns Hopkins University have argued that the impressive reductions in highway fatalities have been more often due to changes in car design than driver behavior. They make the case that the same result can be achieved by altering the design of firearms. Options being developed with regard to personalized or smart guns include:

1. The use of radio frequency identification (RFID) technology with "tags" (e.g. wristwatches, bracelets) containing tiny electromagnetic transmitters that communicate with "readers" embedded in a gun. RFID is widely used for controlled building access, in library book theft prevention, and unlocking and starting cars. When the reader detects the tag, a mechanical device in the gun can move a blocking mechanism so the gun can be fired. Without the tag being in close proximity to the reader on the gun (e.g. the gun is in the possession of an unauthorized user), the blocking mechanism remains in place and the gun is inoperable.

2. Another approach is to use biometric recognition, which scans and recognizes the fingerprint or grip of the authorized user. All of the safety technology is incorporated in the gun itself, and there is no external device or tag that can be lost. For example, with grip recognition, the palm configuration of the owner is recognized after a period of use and the gun will work only when held by the authorized user.

A study conducted by Jon Vernick, codirector of the Center for Gun Policy and Research at the Johns Hopkins Bloomberg School of Public Health, and his associates examined the proportion of unintentional and undetermined firearm-related deaths that might have been prevented had one of three safety devices been in place: personalization devices, loaded chamber indicators showing when a gun is loaded, and magazine safeties that prevent a gun from firing when the ammunition magazine is removed.[89]

The study examined all known unintentional and undetermined firearm deaths from 1991 to 1998 in the state of Maryland and Milwaukee County, Wisconsin. Following a detailed examination of each of the 117 deaths, the researchers found that 44 percent of the deaths could have been prevented by at least one of these safety devices. Deaths involving children (aged 17 years or under) were more likely to be preventable. Based on this study, Vernick and his colleagues estimated that 442 deaths nationwide might have been prevented in 2000 had all guns been equipped with these safety devices. According to researchers at Johns Hopkins, a majority of Americans and four in 10 current gun owners would be willing to buy a gun that operated only in the hands of an authorized user.

The National Institute of Justice (NIJ) produced a report in June 2013 evaluating the readiness of personalized firearm technology.[90] The report revealed that, while personalized guns were not yet available commercially, several prototypes have been created and were "production-ready." At least one personalized handgun system entered the US market in 2013: the Armatix iP1, which includes a handgun and a watch containing a radio frequency identifier that the user must wear to activate the handgun.

Innovative companies include Armatix GmbH, Kodiak Industries, and iGun Technology Corporation. Armatix of Germany, developer of the iP1, a .22 caliber pistol, reports that it has sold its Smart System in Europe and Asia and is seeking approval for commercial sale in the United States. Kodiak Industries of Utah has developed the Intelligun, a fingerprint-based system that unlocks a .45 caliber pistol for immediate operation by authorized users. Kodiak claims a failure rate of 1 in 10,000.

Federal law does not set any safety or design standards for domestically manufactured firearms as firearms and ammunition have been exempted from oversight by the US Consumer Product Safety Commission (CPSC). Therefore, the CPSC presently lacks the authority to require gun manufacturers to produce personalized guns or to otherwise enhance the safety of firearms.

Three states, Maryland, Massachusetts, and New Jersey, have laws dealing with personalization, and they continue to monitor the technology. New Jersey and Massachusetts have gone the farthest to committing their states to personalized guns.

In 2002, New Jersey adopted a law that will at some point require smart gun technology to be incorporated into all handguns available for sale in the state. Twenty-three months after smart handguns are available for commercial sale, the attorney general and the superintendent of state police are mandated to draft a list of personalized handguns that can be sold in the state. Six months after the list of handguns is approved, handguns sold or otherwise transferred in New Jersey will be required to be personalized handguns, with the exception of antique handguns and those used by law enforcement or military personnel. There have been attempts to repeal this law.

The requirements of the 2002 law have not yet been satisfied. In November 2014, New Jersey's Attorney General John Hoffman stated:

> *After careful consideration of the iP1's design, we have determined that it does not satisfy the statutory definition because, as a matter of design, the pistol may be fired by a person who is not an authorized or recognized user. That is, as long as the pistol is situated within 10 inches of the enabling wristwatch, it may be fired by anyone—the authorized user or any other person who is able to pull the trigger. While the system does incorporate a PIN code or a timer to disable the handgun, when the weapon is enabled, there is nothing in the technology which automatically limits its operational use so that it may only be fired by an authorized or recognized user (so long as the pistol is within a 10-inch proximity to the wristwatch component). Situations may readily be envisioned in which an unauthorized individual gains access to the pistol in close enough proximity to the wristwatch component (by either maintaining possession of the pistol within 10 inches of the authorized user's wrist on which he or she is wearing the watch, or by forcibly taking possession of the wristwatch), and therefore would be able to fire the weapon, despite the limiting technology. Accordingly, we are unable to conclude that the iP1 design meets all the elements of New Jersey's statutory definition of a personalized handgun under N.J.S.2C:39-1(dd), and therefore its availability for retail sales purposes will not trigger the operation of N.J.S.2C:58-2.4 (requiring the promulgation of a list of personalized handguns) and N.J.S.2C:58-2.5 (prohibiting the sale of non-personalized handguns).[91]*

The AG's argument in effect declares that guns adopting radio frequency identification technology do not qualify as personalized, which represents an enormous setback to the movement to make safer guns commercially available. Since this is a sweeping rejection of the technology as opposed to a more nuanced critique of the gun's reliability, one is left to wonder if Hoffman, a Republican in Chris Christie's administration, was motivated by an allegiance to special interests rather than the safety of New Jersey residents.

I would argue that a weapon adopting RFID technology is personalized when the owner takes the appropriate precautions to ensure that a child cannot get access to the gun when the enabling watch or ring is within 10 inches of the gun. In any event, a password also must be entered before the gun can fire. As for scenarios in which an aggressor overpowers the owner and gains access to the watch, again the password must be entered, and this will happen far less frequently than that same aggressor seizing a gun without the technology and using it against the owner. All technologies have shortcomings and can be defeated in certain situations. However, given the number of suicides and accidents involving young people, as well as stolen guns subsequently used in crime, it boggles the mind that the New Jersey AG would prefer to keep having so many improperly stored guns without such safety devices as opposed to having them incorporate safety devices that will only infrequently be circumvented.

Massachusetts views personalized gun technology as an alternative to locking devices in its requirement that handguns or large capacity weapons be sold with a safety device in order to prevent the misuse of such a weapon by unauthorized users. The state police must approve any technology or locking device and have not yet done so.

As with pretty well any form of innovation that can enhance public safety, the National Rifle Association and gun rights advocates have resisted even those reforms that would not remove a single gun from the marketplace but would merely prevent deadly accidents and other misuses.[92] The objections to smart gun technologies include price and the fear that the technology will fail when a gun is needed most. There is no disputing the fact that technologies can fail and even guns without personalizing features can fail; however, as indicated above, Johns Hopkins researchers suggest that many more deaths will be prevented with such features than lives will be lost due to the failure of these technologies.

For example, for those with keyless entry to their cars, how often does this fail? The answer is, very infrequently and only when the battery needs to be replaced. The likelihood that a failure will happen when a gun owner is attacked is very remote. More often, the gun, regardless of the presence of personalizing technology, cannot be deployed because attackers do not telegraph their moves. The value of guns for self-defense is greatly exaggerated. For a comprehensive overview of the topic of gun use for the purpose of self-defense, I invite the reader to examine Chapters 9 and 10 in my book, *Confronting Gun Violence in America*.

As this section is being written, there is renewed interest on the part of several companies to develop more reliable and powerful smart guns. Investors are showing greater interest and advocacy groups are placing increasing pressure on gun makers to produce weapons with personalizing technologies.[93]

Recommendations:

- The federal government should monitor progress in the development of personalized firearm technology and create incentives to encourage research, development, and the commercial sale of personalized firearms and gun safety technology. Research should include data on the reliability of existing and emerging technologies.

- The Consumer Product Safety Commission should be empowered to set standards for personalized firearms and to assess the readiness for the civilian market of all new firearm technologies. Testing of personalized weapons should be conducted by a certified independent laboratory.

- A target date should be set for introducing personalized guns into the market.

- Once personalized weapons are approved for the civilian market, law enforcement agencies and the military should be encouraged to purchase personalized guns and buy guns only from companies that make or sell personalized weapons.

Part III

Regulating the Gun Industry

8

Holding the Gun Industry
Accountable for its Harms

A fundamental legal principle is that individuals and businesses are accountable for wrongdoing. By imposing financial consequences, the legal system encourages businesses to reduce harm by making products safer and by disclosing risks associated with their use. For example, major lawsuits in the 1990s by the states forced the tobacco industry to act more responsibly. A settlement valued at billions of dollars helped states recover their substantial expenditures for healthcare costs brought by tobacco products. Lawsuits also allowed the disclosure of damning information about how cigarettes were made and marketed, as well as how these processes were concealed. One of the main conditions of the settlement with the tobacco industry was an agreement not to market cigarettes to youth and to fund a foundation created to find ways to reduce smoking among youth.

Why don't victims of gun violence sue gunmakers and/ or retailers for producing or selling the guns that made a murder or massacre possible? Why don't cities or states sue manufacturers or gun dealers for the medical costs incurred as a result of gun violence? In fact, cities like Chicago and Bridgeport (Connecticut) did file lawsuits, something that alarmed the gun industry. As a result, pressure exerted by the NRA led to the enactment of the *Protection of Lawful Commerce in Arms Act (PLCAA)*, which was signed into law by President George W. Bush in 2005.

Under the *PLCAA*, gun manufacturers are protected from liability and cannot be sued when their products are used to commit acts of violence. Lawsuits are potentially among the most powerful means through which individuals who have been harmed can seek redress and hold the gun industry accountable. At the same time, these legal cases allow members of the public to gain insight into the harmful practices of the industry. Aside from compensating victims of violence, civil litigation can contribute to positive change in the gun industry, including decisions to stop marketing weapons and accessories that enable massacres (e.g. military-style weapons and bump stocks) and to incorporate safety features in the design of firearms (e.g. loaded chamber indicators and magazine safeties).

The *PLCAA* has given the gun industry unprecedented immunity from negligence-based lawsuits not enjoyed by any other industry. Specifically, this act shields the industry from lawsuits relating to the use of firearms and ammunition when "the product functioned as designed and intended." The *Act* provides broad protection to companies in the gun industry that make unsafe products and engage in distribution practices that result in easy access by criminals.

For example, after the 2017 mass shooting in Las Vegas, where hundreds were shot by a sniper in a hotel room, victims sued the concert and hotel but could not sue the manufacturers of his guns. It has been noted that gun manufacturers and customers get the benefits of buying and selling guns without bearing any of the costs. The costs are borne by the victims and jurisdictions that provide medical and other services to them, especially in the case of the uninsured. The current legal environment encourages recklessness by the gun industry.

One effect of *PLCAA* is to give legal protection to gun dealers who adopt irresponsible practices.[94] In one case, a gun dealer escaped accountability after selling a gun without a background check to a mentally unstable individual. Although the dealer was so grossly negligent that he sold hundreds of guns without background checks and had his license revoked for willful violations of gun laws, he was allowed to argue that the *PLCAA* prohibited ordinary negligence claims.

One illustration of what appropriate regulation and smart policies might achieve can be seen in relation to road deaths. Over the last century, there has been a 95 percent reduction in car deaths per 100 million miles driven due to the correction of car defects, seatbelts, airbags, speed limits, licensing, insurance, road design (barriers, medians, lighting), and tougher measures to deal with impaired driving.[95]

Repealing the *PLCAA* will create financial consequences for the industry, especially after a large-scale shooting. The gunmaker involved may pay out tens of millions of dollars in costs and damages to victims and their families. This may encourage at least some manufacturers to stop producing weapons capable of these massacres and other businesses may cease to import and sell these guns. Therefore, removing the law that shields the industry from liability may succeed in reducing the supply of military-style weapons.

The reduction in supply and higher insurance premiums should increase the price of these firearms, placing these firearms out of reach to many prospective owners. (Owners, too, may be required to purchase insurance when purchasing firearms.) Exposure of the industry to potential suits may also encourage it to make and sell guns with more safety features that will reduce unauthorized access to guns and the harms (crimes, suicides, and accidents) associated with such access. As mentioned, safety features like seatbelts and airbags in cars have made an enormous difference in reducing deaths and serious injuries.

Aside from repealing the *PLCAA*, a bill is needed to help victims with medical and other costs. Gunmakers can be required to contribute to a fund that pays for health services associated with gunshot wounds and other victim costs, such as compensation for loss of income.[96] Such a fund has been created in the chemical industry. Nationally, there are thousands of contaminated sites due to the dumping of hazardous waste. These sites include manufacturing facilities, processing plants, landfills, and mining sites.[97] In the late 1970s, some of these sites received national attention when the public learned about the risks to human health and the environment.

As a result, Congress established the *Comprehensive Environmental Response, Compensation and Liability Act (CERCLA)* in 1980, also known as Superfund. The *Act* forces the parties responsible for the contamination to either perform cleanups or reimburse the government for EPA-led cleanup work. Where responsibility cannot be determined or a company is unable to pay for the cleanup, Superfund gives EPA the funds and authority to clean up contaminated sites. Most of the funding originally came from a tax on the petroleum and chemical industries, although most of it now comes from taxpayers.

A special tax on the gun industry or on all firearm transactions may support a similar fund to support victims, health systems, or communities wrestling with the costs of gun violence. A process can be established whereby injured parties and their families can make claims to offset some of their expenses. The tax also would make firearms more expensive, potentially reducing the number of guns in circulation. The industry would have an incentive to behave responsibly in order to cut down the size of its contribution to the fund as the tax could be adjusted up or down depending on the number of claims. This approach establishes a market solution as a possible alternative to banning weapons, which is more difficult to achieve due to political challenges.

New York is holding the gun industry accountable in another way. In 2018, state regulators fined 10 insurance companies a total of five million dollars for underwriting the NRA's self-defense insurance programs.[98] For example, the NRA's Carry Guard insurance program reimburses the legal expenses and other costs associated with shooting people in self-defense. Critics branded this as "murder insurance," and New York argues that it is unlawful to insure actions that go beyond the use of reasonable force.

Recommendations:

- The *Protection of Lawful Commerce in Arms Act* should be repealed.

- A special tax on all firearm transactions should be created to help offset the costs of gun violence to victims, health systems, and communities.

- All states should examine insurance products that may potentially protect individuals who use guns to engage in unlawful uses of force.

9

Protecting Consumers and Inspecting Dealers

The Consumer Product Safety Commission (CPSC) is the federal agency that ensures that consumer products are safe. The CPSC regulates flammability standards for mattresses, and it estimates that 270 lives are saved each year. It also regulates children's toys, appliances, and all sorts of household products in order to protect the public from harm.

However, unlike virtually every consumer product manufactured and sold in the US, the CPSC has been expressly forbidden by Congress from regulating firearms or ammunition. This was prompted by the fear of some legislators that allowing the CPSC to regulate guns would create a slippery slope leading to the disarming of Americans. Consequently, no federal agency has the authority to oversee the design of firearms to ensure they do not cause harm as a result of defects, even as more than 100,000 Americans are killed or injured by gunfire each year.

Regulations might require equipping guns with trigger locks and chamber indicators, as well as personalizing guns so that only lawful owners can use them. Such measures could help prevent crimes by unauthorized users, accidental deaths, and suicides by family members of gun owners. In addition, regulations can ensure that firearms are made with high-quality materials so they are reliable and meet minimum safety standards (e.g. ensuring that weapons are not structurally weakened when fired or discharge when dropped).

Many guns used in crime and mass shootings are obtained from licensed dealers. Often, purchases are made through "straw purchasers," individuals with clean criminal records who buy guns on behalf of those who would be ineligible to do so due to a felony conviction or some other disqualifying condition. Some dealers are especially prolific in selling guns that are eventually used in crime. A 2000 report by the Bureau of Alcohol, Tobacco, Firearms and Explosives (ATF) revealed that just over 1 percent of federally licensed firearm dealers sold 57 percent of the guns later traced to crime.[99] For example, in 2005, 447 guns used in crimes were traced to a sporting goods store outside of Oakland, California. An astounding one of every eight guns sold in that store were later found to be used in a crime or were seized from an individual involved in crime.[100]

Gun shows are another major source of guns used in crimes. According to the ATF, 30 percent of guns involved in federal gun trafficking investigations have a gun show connection.[101] New York City investigators visited seven gun shows in Nevada, Ohio, and Tennessee.[102] They conducted integrity tests of 47 sellers, both licensed dealers and private sellers. Nearly two-thirds of private sellers approached by investigators failed the integrity test, selling weapons to buyers who said they probably could not pass background checks. Some private sellers failed this test more than once at different shows. While private sellers are not required to conduct background checks, they are committing a felony if they know or have reason to believe they are selling to a prohibited purchaser.

More than nine out of 10 licensed dealers also failed the integrity test by selling to apparent straw purchasers. In all, 35 out of 47 sellers approached by investigators completed sales to people who appeared to be criminals or straw purchasers. Investigators also learned that some private sellers were in the business of selling guns without a license. For example, one seller sold to investigators at three different shows and admitted to selling 348 assault rifles in less than one year.

In America, there are more licensed gun dealers than grocery stores or McDonald's restaurants.[103] Major flaws in federal gun laws impede the ATF from preventing the illegal diversion of firearms from licensed firearm dealers. The agency is limited to one unannounced inspection of a dealer in any year, and it faces an uphill battle in convicting dealers of wrongdoing. In criminal cases, it must show that the dealer *willfully* engaged in wrongdoing, and to revoke a license a pattern of wrongdoing over many years must be demonstrated.[104] Missing records can hide illegal sales; however, serious recordkeeping violations usually go unpunished. Since 1986, recordkeeping violations have been classified as misdemeanors rather than felonies. Federal prosecutors generally spend limited time prosecuting misdemeanors so most recordkeeping violations escape punishment.

The ATF simply lacks the resources to monitor the thousands of gun dealers across the country. The Department of Justice's Office of the Inspector General concluded that it would take the ATF more than 22 years to inspect all federally licensed dealers.[105] A *Washington Post* investigation found that due to inadequate staffing, ATF inspects the average dealer just once a decade.[106] The paper also reported that there are only about 15 license revocations in a typical year. Moreover, the Inspector General's 2013 report found that some license revocation processes took more than two years to complete, allowing scofflaw dealers to legally continue selling firearms during that time. The report also found that between 2004 and 2011 licensed gun dealers reported 174,679 firearms missing from their inventories, which is a major concern considering these guns may end up being used in crimes.

Gun shows are another weak link in the firearms marketplace. According to a report by the ATF, there are about 4,000 such shows a year in the US, as well as numerous other public markets (e.g., flea markets) at which firearms are sold or traded.[107] Currently, under federal law, private sellers are not required to find out whether they are selling a gun to a felon or other prohibited person. If these firearms are recovered at a crime scene, it is very difficult to trace them back to the purchaser.

The ATF report notes:

> *The casual atmosphere in which firearms are sold at gun shows provides an opportunity for individual buyers and sellers to exchange firearms without the expense of renting a table, and it is not uncommon to see people walking around a show attempting to sell a firearm. They may sell their firearms to a vendor who has rented a table or simply to someone they meet at the show. Many non-*

licensees entice potential customers to their tables with comments such as, "No background checks required"... too often the shows provide a ready supply of firearms to prohibited persons, gangs, violent criminals, and illegal firearms traffickers.[108]

The oversight seen in most industries has been virtually absent in relation to the gun industry and its products. Guns are exempted from consumer laws, and the industry is shielded from liability relating to harms associated with its products. Both federal law and inadequate resources limit the ATF's inspections of gun dealers. Also, at least a quarter of all gun sales occur in the unregulated private market.

Reporter Nicholas Kristof of *The New York Times* has pointed out how regulation and other preventive measures succeeded in reducing deaths from car accidents and that a public health approach also should be applied to reducing gun deaths:

Over the decades, we have systematically taken steps to make cars safer. We adopted seatbelts and airbags, limited licenses for teenage drivers, cracked down on drunken driving and established roundabouts and better crosswalks, auto safety inspections and rules about texting while driving. This approach has been stunningly successful. We have reduced the fatality rate by more than 95 percent.[109]

A study by Mayors Against Illegal Guns found that states that do not require gun dealer inspections tend to export guns used in crime to other states at a rate that is 50 percent greater than states that do permit or require such inspections.[110] States with less regulation of dealers are also more likely to be the source of trafficked guns, as determined by the time it takes for a gun to be used in crimes following the initial purchase—two years or less is deemed to be an indication of trafficking. Another study found that state laws allowing or requiring inspections of gun dealers were associated with significantly lower firearm homicide rates than states without these regulations.[111]

Law enforcement operations against dealers in New York City illustrate how effective enforcement can alter dealer behavior, reducing the number of guns that are eventually used in crime. In 2006, the city launched a number of undercover operations and lawsuits, which could proceed under the *Protection of Lawful Commerce in Arms Act* if the dealer knowingly violated laws dealing with gun sales. Investigators identified 55 gun dealers in seven states who were supplying guns used in crimes in the city. About half of these dealers were caught facilitating illegal sales in an undercover operation and were subsequently sued by the city. Nearly all the defendants settled their case and agreed to modify their business practices. An analysis focusing on 10 of these dealers found that the change in their practices was followed by an 84 percent reduction in the likelihood that a gun sold by one of them would be later recovered in a New York crime.[112]

Recommendations:

- The ATF should have the authority and funding necessary to conduct routine inspections of gun dealers at its discretion. The agency should not be limited to one inspection per year.

- Sellers of ammunition should be required to obtain a license.

- *The Protection of Lawful Commerce in Arms Act,* which grants virtual immunity to the gun industry from negligence-based lawsuits, should be repealed.

- Aside from penalties levied against gunmakers and dealers for violating laws and compromising public safety, policies should be developed that reward manufacturers and gun sellers for engaging in behaviors that promote public safety and reduce gun trafficking (e.g. through publicity and the awarding of federal or state contracts). These behaviors include selling guns with safety features that exceed federal or state requirements, curbing sales to unscrupulous dealers, and adopting measures to prevent gun sales to those likely to engage in crime or the trafficking of firearms.

- Federal legislation that restricts the release of firearms trace data should be repealed to facilitate criminal investigations and to permit research on gun trafficking patterns.

- Limiting the number of firearms an individual can buy at one time can potentially prevent an individual bent on mass murder from quickly acquiring an arsenal of weapons. Such a law can also make it more difficult for those engaged in gun trafficking. A policy of one firearm per 30 days should be adopted at the federal level. Gun collectors may be exempted if they can prove they are *bona fide* collectors and that the guns have been deactivated.

Part IV

Changing Violent Norms

10

Repealing Laws that Encourage Violence

A majority of states have some version of a Stand Your Ground (SYG) law. While they vary, these laws tend to give individuals the right to use deadly force when they have a "reasonable belief" that they are facing death or serious injury. Under these laws, no actual attack is necessary to justify the use of force, including lethal force. A person who has provoked someone or instigated a conflict and uses lethal force may still be granted immunity from prosecution if the person they have provoked responds violently to the provocation. A detailed *Tampa Bay Times* analysis of 200 Florida SYG cases found that, in nearly a third of the cases, defendants initiated the fight, shot an unarmed person, or pursued their victims—and still went free.[113]

Under SYG laws, there is no duty to retreat or to solve a dispute in a nonviolent manner. For centuries under English law, people could not justify the use of lethal force unless they could prove that they could not preserve themselves in any other way. Critics refer to these laws as "shoot first" laws. The *Tampa Bay Times* study showed that in 79 percent of the cases the shooter could have retreated to avoid the confrontation.

Widespread gun carrying and a low level of firearms training in many states, along with SYG laws, form a toxic brew. SYG legitimizes and enables the use of lethal violence, and widespread gun carrying ensures that many citizens have access to lethal weapons when disputes arise. SYG emboldens people to act like vigilantes rather than to solve disputes nonviolently because they believe they will be immune from prosecution.

Justifiable homicides in Florida tripled following the introduction of SYG in 2005.[114] In 2016, the *American Medical Association's Internal Medicine Journal* published a study showing that Florida's SYG law was associated with a 24 percent increase in homicides and a 32 percent increase in firearm-related homicides.[115] It is estimated that an additional 4,200 people were murdered with a gun in Florida in the 10-year period following enactment of SYG.[116] Texas A&M researchers have found that homicide rates in 21 states with a SYG law increased by an average of 8 percent over other states or 600 more homicides per year in those states alone.[117] Furthermore, this study found that SYG laws did *not* deter crimes such as robbery and aggravated assault.

John Roman, a Senior Fellow at the Urban Institute, analyzed data from the FBI Supplemental Homicide Reports to conduct a comparative analysis of justified homicide rates from 2005 to 2010 in SYG and non-SYG states.[118] Although racial disparities are also found in states without SYG laws, these disparities were significantly greater in SYG states. In these states, a white shooter who kills a black victim is 350 percent more likely to be found to be justified in the killing than if the same shooter killed a white victim. In these states, justifiable shooting rulings ranged from 3 percent to 15 percent for white-on-white, black-on-white, and black-on-black killings. When the shooter was white and the victim black, 36 percent were ruled justified.

Overall, the evidence shows that SYG laws increase homicide rates and do not act as a deterrent to crime. They have also been found to be applied inequitably depending upon the race of the shooter and victim.

Recommendations:

- States should conduct rigorous evaluations of SYG laws to determine their impact on homicide, their deterrent effect (if any), and whether they are applied in a racially equitable manner.

- States should consider repealing these laws if they are associated with increases in violence or are implemented in a discriminatory way.

- Based on currently available information, these laws should be repealed in their entirety.

11

Deterring Violence in High-Risk Neighborhoods

Operation Ceasefire

Efforts to reduce gun violence are not limited to the regulation of guns or the firearms industry. Aggressive law enforcement strategies that target high-risk individuals or neighborhoods also have been shown to be effective. Rather than engaging in routine preventive patrols and responding to crimes and calls for service, focused deterrence strategies first assess the nature and dynamics that contribute to a neighborhood's gun violence problems. Then, a strategy that combines law enforcement, community mobilization, and social service measures is developed. Focused deterrence operations adopt the following general approach in the affected area:

- An interagency enforcement group is formed comprising police, probation and parole agencies, and prosecutors.

- Key offenders and groups/gangs are identified.

- A customized enforcement operation is directed at these offenders and groups to influence their behavior through the use of available legal tools.

- These enforcement operations are complemented by providing services and making appeals to these individuals and groups to refrain from violent behavior.

- Face-to-face meetings are set up with at-risk individuals and groups during which they are told what they can do to avoid legal consequences.[119]

First implemented in Boston's Operation Ceasefire project, a working group of criminal justice, social service, and community-based agencies, in partnership with Harvard University researchers, diagnosed the youth gun violence problem in Boston as one of patterned, largely vendetta-like conflicts among a small population of chronic offenders.[120] These groups were responsible for more than 60 percent of youth homicides in the city. Law enforcement agencies sought to disrupt street drug activity, focused on low-level street crimes such as trespassing, served outstanding warrants, recruited confidential informants, enforced probation and parole conditions strictly, requested stronger bail terms, and brought potentially severe federal investigative and prosecutorial attention to gang-related drug and gun activity.

At the same time, outreach workers, probation and parole officers, and community groups offered services to gang members and delivered the message that violence was unacceptable. This message was transmitted in formal meetings between police, correctional, and/or gang workers. The focused deterrence approach simultaneously emphasizes the risk of reoffending and the importance of decreasing opportunities for violence and strengthening communities. Targeted offenders are to be treated with respect and dignity, an approach that research shows makes it more likely that citizens will behave in a law-abiding fashion.

Evaluations of focused deterrence strategies have generally found large reductions in violent crime. Boston experienced a 63 percent reduction in youth homicides, Stockton (California) experienced a 42 percent reduction in gun homicides, and New Haven (Connecticut) saw shootings decline by 73 percent.[121]

Hot Spots Policing

Criminologists have learned that routine police patrols are not very effective since they cover an entire area equally—although crime is not distributed equally—and are spread too thinly to make much of a difference. This approach of just cruising through an area rarely intercepts crimes in progress, serves as a minimal deterrent due to the small number of passes by any location, and generally just reassures citizens that law enforcement officers are there for them. Patrick Vincent Murphy, the visionary police chief of New York, Detroit, and Washington, DC, once said that preventive patrol does not prevent crime but merely reassures the citizen that the police department exists, much like the city zoo.

A new approach complements routine patrols with an intensive focus on highly active neighborhoods, blocks, or even smaller sites (e.g., bus terminals). These "hot spots" are identified through crime mapping. Police officers are deployed to these areas in greater numbers and engage in crime suppression activities, as well as efforts to deal with the underlying causes of crime at that location. For example, in 2009, the Philadelphia Police Department participated in an experiment in which foot patrols were deployed in pairs to the most troublesome intersections in the city. Officers talked to residents, visited juvenile hangouts, and stopped known lawbreakers in their cars and on sidewalks.

In the program's first three months, there was a 23 percent reduction in reported violent crime in comparison with control areas—i.e. those areas not receiving the foot patrols.[122] While there was some increase in violent crime in zones surrounding the target areas, the reduction in crime was greater than that displaced to other areas. In the areas targeted by the experiment, enforcement actions (arrests, pedestrian and vehicle stops, disruptions of disturbances, and narcotics enforcement) increased, likely deterring violence. However, once the experiment was over and the foot patrols were removed from the crime hot spots, there were no longer significant differences in violence between these spots and areas that served as controls—indicating the impact of the foot patrols was not sustained once they were removed.

Gun Squads

Another approach to hot spots policing is the formation of gun squads designed to get illegal weapons off the streets of especially violent neighborhoods. These specialized squads use intelligence to identify individuals who may possess illegal weapons. They encourage community members to provide tips on individuals who may be carrying illegally and they frequently stop individuals and cars to search them for weapons. Over a 29-week period in Kansas City, gun seizures increased by 65 percent and gun crimes, including homicides, fell by 49 percent without pushing crime into adjacent neighborhoods.[123]

Cure Violence

Cure Violence, a nongovernmental program implemented in dozens of American cities, adopts a public health strategy to violence reduction by adopting methods used in disease control. The program seeks to detect and interrupt conflicts, identify and treat those individuals at greatest risk to commit violence, and change social norms conducive to violence. It seeks to identify situations that have a high likelihood of resulting in violence, including retaliatory violence or the release of a high-profile gang member from prison. Workers must have credibility with those they are seeking to influence and meet with participants several times a week, including at critical times of need. They develop a relationship and work to address issues faced by participants, such as education, employment, criminal justice, mental health, substance abuse, and reentry issues through the utilization of existing social services. Workers and volunteers respected by participants discourage the use of violence through educational materials such as posters and fliers.

Cure Violence's website claims that their program has been shown to be successful in reducing shootings, violent confrontations, and homicides in many jurisdictions, with reductions of up to 70 percent. The approach is listed as promising, but independent evaluations have so far found the results to be uneven. It is, however, cost efficient, placing a low level of demand on law enforcement and criminal justice system resources.[124]

Recommendations:

- Communities should support innovative programs that identify high-risk individuals and neighborhoods and that offer a combination of focused strategies to deter lawbreaking and support to these individuals.

- Strong penalties should be imposed on individuals using guns in crime, as well as those engaged in firearms trafficking and straw purchases.

- Aside from strong penalties, messages delivered by program staff, public service announcements, and school programs should all send messages promoting nonviolent conflict resolution and the unacceptability of violence as a means of settling disputes and dealing with personal problems.

Part V
Citizen Initiatives

12

Voluntary and Nongovernmental Initiatives

Many people have asked what they can do to make a difference in relation to gun violence. People understandably feel powerless and believe that the NRA's obstructionism is insurmountable. However, independent of efforts to change laws, it is worth considering nongovernmental and voluntary measures and programs that can protect the public from gun violence. Voluntary programs are those run by volunteers and/or those in which participation on the part of the public is voluntary rather than mandated by law.

With a group of committed volunteers, the support of local agencies, and perhaps some limited fundraising, these programs can be launched without delay and impose little or no burden on public agencies. And because they are voluntary and require no change in the law, they cannot be derailed by opponents of proposed legislation designed to prevent gun injuries and deaths. Voluntary, grassroots initiatives also can raise awareness of the benefits of safe practices and empower those who want to take action, no matter how modest, to make their communities safer.

Some measures require paid staff but still fall outside the public sector.

Here are some examples:

Securing Guns in the Home

Close to five million American children live in homes with loaded, unlocked firearms. Inadequately stored guns contribute to teenage suicides and violence, deadly accidents among children, and gun thefts. School shooters often obtain their guns from their home or that of a relative.[125] There are no federal laws in the US requiring the safe storage of firearms and just one state, Massachusetts, requires all firearms to be stored with a lock in place.

In Broward County, Florida, attorney Barbara Markley and fellow members of the Gun Safety Committee of the League of Women Voters (LWV) initiated Lock It Up, a program that is rapidly gaining more partners. League members learned that the Veterans Administration maintains a large inventory of trigger locks due to the elevated suicide risk of veterans. The VA has donated thousands of locks to the LWV, which is distributing them to a wide variety of agencies and professionals: Law enforcement, municipalities, libraries, churches, pediatricians, family therapy and university clinics, and daycare centers. They also have produced a brochure to raise awareness about the dangers of unlocked guns around children and teens.

Gun Buybacks

Gun buybacks allow people to turn in guns, usually to the police, for cash or gift cards with no questions asked. They provide the public an opportunity to turn in weapons that are not being used, are possessed illegally, or that may be a danger to households. In some cases, hundreds of guns have been turned in. Most initiatives involve law enforcement agencies, which receive the guns, and some partner with physicians and medical centers that can counsel gun owners about safety.

Evaluations of voluntary gun buybacks tend to show that they do not reduce gun violence because the number of guns turned in makes up just a small proportion of all guns in the community.[126] However, proponents argue that some violence or suicides may be prevented. They also say buybacks encourage people to consider the risks posed by guns in the home and enable owners to adopt safer practices with firearms since participants may interact with police and medical personnel when they turn in their guns. At a recent event in Hillsborough County, Florida, the Sheriff's Office received 1,173 guns in five hours, including some stolen guns.[127] At a previous event in that county, 2,541 guns had been turned in.

Consumer and Investor Activism

Consumers can pressure stores to refrain from selling military-style and other highly lethal weapons through letter-writing campaigns, personal appeals to store managers and executives, social media campaigns on Facebook and Twitter, and boycotts. Individuals and pension funds also can refuse to buy and divest from gun stocks or mutual funds containing gun stocks until those companies stop selling military-style weapons and start producing weapons with certain safety features (e.g. magazine safeties, loaded chamber indicators) and personalized (smart) weapons.

Also, through their elected representatives, individuals can pressure the military and police to stop buying guns from companies that do not incorporate safety features. Forty percent of all gun industry revenues are derived from government contracts. In October 2018, the mayor of Toledo, Ohio announced that his city will enter into contracts only with "responsible" gun companies—in other words, companies that do not sell or make assault-style weapons, require that dealers conduct background checks, invest in gun and ammunition-tracing technologies, and adopt industry best practices for inventory control and transactions.[128]

Given the targeting of several campuses by mass shooters, some academics are demanding that their retirement funds be "gun-free."[129] In one initiative, more than 4,000 faculty members threatened a firm managing their funds with the transfer of their money to gun-free funds if they continued to invest in companies that manufacture assault-style weapons.

Driven by outrage over the massacre at Marjory Stoneman Douglas High School in Parkland and backed by some of America's largest institutional investors, Sister Judy Byron of Seattle and a small group of shareholders have forced two gun manufacturers, Sturm Ruger and American Outdoor Brands, to produce reports detailing the use of their guns in violent crimes and showing what steps the companies are taking to develop safer weapons.[130] Although the companies urged their shareholders to reject the proposals, a majority sided with the activists.

Byron persuaded the Adrian Dominicans, a Catholic religious institute, to buy gun stocks and organized other members of the Interfaith Center on Corporate

Responsibility to join her, pooling their holdings in three companies: The retailer Dick's Sporting Goods and the two above-mentioned manufacturers. Following the Parkland shooting, large investors in the companies joined Byron's effort, which gave them the votes to pass the measures at Sturm Ruger and American Outdoor Brands. While the companies are not required to follow the resolutions to change their operations, it is expected they will comply rather than risk shareholders' anger. Byron appealed to the companies to not only seek profitable returns for investors but also to mitigate the adverse impacts of their products.

Protest Actions

In the era of Donald Trump, protest actions have become common, ranging from countless rallies to the occupation of government buildings and offices, with the largest nationwide protest occurring on March 24, 2018 when high school students led millions of Americans in the March for Our Lives. Evidence indicates that enthusiasm has been growing for meaningful gun policy reforms since the Parkland shooting. At Stanford University, 2,500 doctors and nurses marched for action on gun violence, demanding more research, and training to deal with the national crisis.

Supporting Victims of Abuse

A significant amount of gun violence and the majority of mass shootings have a domestic violence connection. Many women killed with a gun are shot by a domestic partner. Programs that empower women to take action if they are in an abusive relationship may keep the relationship from escalating to serious violence. Especially dangerous is the post-separation period, and a fear of violence often keeps women from exiting dangerous relationships. Programs that offer victims shelter or support while they remain in their own homes can be empowering and help keep them safe.

For example, the REACH program in Massachusetts has an Emergency Shelter Program providing crisis intervention and support services for victims of domestic violence who are not safe in their own home.[131] Services include assistance with finding longer-term housing, support with legal issues, and access to other resources to help families heal physically and emotionally. REACH's Community-Based Advocacy Program offers a similar range of services to domestic violence survivors who do not want to leave an abusive relationship or who are not seeking shelter. The charitable organization also can help with safety planning, finding a job or housing, or accessing benefits.

Public Education Initiatives

Educating the public about gun safety prevention can include offering them tips for making their homes safer (e.g. securing guns with trigger locks or other locking devices) and the steps they need to take to protect their children when visiting the homes of gun owners. Safety presentations, videos, written materials on gun violence and safety, and PSAs can shift public opinion, especially when done on a large scale. One example is the League of Women Voters, an advocacy group run by volunteers that presents educational forums on gun safety, lobbies legislators, makes appearances on television and radio, and reaches out to the public in a variety of other ways.

Over the last three decades, the gun lobby has been successful in selling the idea that guns make us safer from violence. Pew Research Center reports that just 34 percent of Americans said in 1993 that it was more important to protect gun rights than to control gun ownership, but by 2014 some of its polling showed that the number had climbed to 52 percent. Recently, in the aftermath of several large-scale mass shootings, opinion is shifting once again in favor of gun control.[132] Increasing grassroots activity, including educational efforts on the part of groups favoring tighter regulation of guns may be a factor. Thoughtful and evidence-based letters to the editor and other media commentary also can have a cumulative effect on public opinion.

Mobilizing the Community

In many targeted school attacks, information was available regarding the shooter's preparations. The most notable case was that of Nikolas Cruz, the young man who committed the atrocity at Marjory Stoneman Douglas High School in Parkland. Cruz was the subject of dozens of 9-1-1 calls to law enforcement and two separate tips to the FBI.[133] He also came to the attention of the Florida Department of Children and Families and was well known in the community and in school for violent behavior, including threats made with guns and his desire to be a school shooter.

Many school shooters have a history of depression, suicide attempts, or suicidal thoughts. In more than three-quarters of the school attacks studied by the US Secret Service, at least one person—usually a friend, schoolmate, or sibling—had information that the attacker was contemplating or planning the attack and, in the majority of cases, more than one person was aware of the impending attack. In addition, before nearly all the school attacks, the perpetrators exhibited behavior that caused others—school officials, parents, teachers, police, fellow students—to be concerned. All of the above reinforces the need for schools and communities to set up mechanisms to encourage those with information of a possible attack to come forward.

It is a serious mistake to simply expel troubled kids. Cruz and Adam Lanza, the shooter at Sandy Hook Elementary School in Newtown (Connecticut), were loners who fell through the cracks of the mental health and educational systems. Cruz was expelled for his behavior and left to his own resources following the death of his mother. Social isolation is a factor in many mass shootings and, whether it is a cause or effect of the disturbing behavior, it is in our collective interest to intervene and monitor the behavior of highly alienated individuals who exhibit threatening behavior. Sandy Hook Promise, an organization founded by family members of victims of the mass shooting in Newtown, funds a program that helps students develop the social-emotional skills to reach out to other students and include those who may be chronically isolated in order to create a culture of inclusion and connectedness in school and the community.[134] The program is funded through charitable donations and products sold with the Sandy Hook Promise label on them.

Making a Donation

Individuals seeking to make a difference can make a donation to a variety of initiatives. Donations can be made to a university or foundation to support gun violence research as well as to any number of activist groups, such as Moms Demand Action, the Brady Campaign to Prevent

Gun Violence, or Giffords. Donations also can be made to a local trauma center or a program aiding victims of violence, including domestic violence. In addition, it's important to contribute to political candidates running on strong anti-gun violence platforms.

Voting for Change in Gun Policies

One of the easiest steps people can take to effect change is to vote. Informed voters can support candidates who are committed to serious legal reforms. There are indications that the electorate is quite enthusiastic regarding the gun issue, a departure from the past when it was largely gun owners who were focused on gun policy. One useful tool to determine where candidates stand on guns is gunsensevoter.org. On that site, the large grassroots group Moms Demand Action for Gun Sense in America endorses candidates who support laws shown to be effective in combating gun violence.

Part VI

Policy Lessons from the Field

13

Lesson #1: The Merits of a Comprehensive Approach to Violence Prevention

School Shootings

America has a mass shooting and school shooting problem that stands out significantly when compared with other advanced countries.[135] Following the mass shooting at Marjory Stoneman Douglas High School in Parkland, there were calls for improved school security. While enhancing school security is a legitimate short-term measure in keeping students safe, it falls seriously short of a comprehensive approach to the problem. Targeted school attacks were exceedingly rare prior to 1992 when school security was a low priority.[136] Armed security, active shooter drills, and lockdown procedures, all of which are routine in public schools today, were unheard of prior to the 1990s. Thus, security vulnerabilities alone cannot account for the recent surge in school shootings because schools typically adopt far more security measures than in the past. Something else must be driving the recent surge.

Harvard political scientist Robert Putnam has shown that 18- to 29-year-olds are becoming more disengaged from community life. Church attendance, participation in public meetings, and political activities have all declined sharply from the 1970s.[137] Young people spend more time alone than they did decades ago and spend an inordinate amount of time using electronic devices. Those experiencing some form of crisis are less likely to lean on family, places of worship, or social organizations given weaker ties to these institutions.

Depression among young people has increased dramatically and there was a 50 percent increase in suicide among 15- to 24-year-olds between 1999 and 2014.[138] This is the age group most at risk to commit school attacks. Nearly eight in 10 school attackers exhibited a history of suicide attempts or suicidal thoughts prior to their attack, and more than half had a recorded history of feeling extremely depressed or desperate.[139] There is a significant pool of alienated and depressed young people who may experience despair following a major event, such as expulsion from school, loss of a relationship, ostracism by peers, or bullying.

A US Secret Service study showed that many school attackers are members of a fringe group or are viewed as loners. A significant number have a history of suspensions or expulsions from school. Many have been bullied or attacked, in some cases over a long period. The Secret Service's study identified a number of cases in which the experience of being bullied had a significant impact on the shooter and appeared to be a factor in the decision to launch an attack against a school.

Virtually all mass murderers or school attackers have experienced a major loss prior to the attack, including a perceived failure or loss of status, loss of a loved one, a major illness suffered by the attacker or someone significant to him, or the loss of a significant relationship, including a romantic one. Often, others were aware the perpetrator was considering a school attack, encouraged an attack, and/or noticed disturbing behavior. These findings point to many opportunities for intervention and vigilance on the part of schools, community groups, and law enforcement.

While most depressed individuals, loners, and members of fringe groups will not launch attacks, a caring, cohesive, and effective community can intervene positively in assisting those who are experiencing a personal crisis. We need to ask why school officials, family members, and peers who were often aware of the danger failed to intervene in some way to avert violence. To successfully prevent some attacks, the surrounding community must recognize the signs of danger, care enough to act on those signs, and allocate the necessary resources and legal tools to provide support to individuals in need.

Coinciding with the trend toward increasing social isolation, there is greater access to weapons designed for combat that can fire highly lethal, high-velocity bullets rapidly and when equipped with high capacity magazines, can allow a shooter to discharge up to 100 rounds without reloading. The Parkland shooter obtained his AR-15 legally when he was 18, despite numerous disturbing actions and calls to law enforcement. In two-thirds of school shootings, perpetrators have acquired unsecured weapons from their homes or the residences of a relative or friend.[140] The combination of a large pool of at-risk youth and easy access to highly lethal weapons is a recipe for the mass shootings that we've seen.

Many schools around the country already have adopted some basic security measures. In Florida, after the Parkland mass shooting, $100 million was allocated for school security statewide, or about $25,000 per public school. This may be enough to install about a dozen security doors in classrooms but it does not approach what is needed. (Added to this, there are numerous other "soft" targets for shooters, including theaters, shopping malls, clubs, airports, and stadiums. Securing schools alone fails to address the risks to which other people are exposed and may place other targets at increased risk as perpetrators seek less fortified targets.)

A serious effort to enhance school security involves access control protocols (screening all who enter a school in the morning and at lunch time, where applicable), surveillance through monitored cameras and patrols, adequate perimeter security, intrusion detection systems, security doors and bullet-resistant windows, adequately trained and properly armed security personnel, emergency communications, and lockdown procedures. Turning schools into prison-like facilities is prohibitively expensive, creates more fear and disruption for teachers and staff, and fundamentally alters the learning environment. Resources also are inevitably drawn from educational budgets. In the unlikely event we went down this path, we would only mitigate risk in relation to one type of soft target—schools.

We need to address the social isolation and other factors that drive school shooters, along with the easy access to weapons capable of mass slaughter. A number of cities have developed school dropout reengagement centers to identify high school dropouts or chronic truants and work closely with them to provide the mentoring and other support required to complete their degrees and to meet their vocational needs.[141] For example, the program created after the Newtown shooting and funded by Sandy Hook Promise helps students develop the social-emotional skills to reach out to and include those who may be chronically isolated in order to create a culture of inclusion and connectedness in school and the community.[142]

A Note on Arming Teachers

The gun lobby has promoted the idea that teachers and other school staff receive training and carry guns as a means of protecting schools from gunmen. Following the Parkland massacre, Florida embraced such a program and offered funding for school districts wishing to adopt it.

Surveys show that teachers, school safety experts, law enforcement, and the public oppose the idea.[143] Like their college and university counterparts, most educators are not interested in doubling as security guards, and students would feel less safe with schools awash in guns. Teachers worry about undermining their special role as educators and mentors, which consists of a different skill set from that of security staff. School teachers are usually women, who tend to have low gun ownership levels. Schools would likely lose valuable talent. Even if only a few teachers were armed, incentives would likely be required to recruit and retain teachers with armed training, creating a preference for those prepared to undergo the necessary training over talent in the classroom. In addition, scarce educational resources will be diverted from the classroom to firearms training.

The cost of training teachers and/or other school staff willing to serve as armed marshals would be prohibitive, and ongoing training and recertification would require time out of class with its associated costs. Kansas gave school districts the prerogative of arming teachers, and the state's largest insurer of schools refused to cover schools with armed instructors, deeming the situation as unduly risky.[144]

In general, the training required of people with permits to carry guns, in states where a permit is required, is woefully inadequate. Rigorous training ought to include instruction in the law pertaining to the use of force, gun safety and handling, judgment (when to shoot and not to shoot), awareness of the possibility of friendly fire incidents, and marksmanship under stress. Even trained police officers miss their targets about 80 percent of the time in combat situations. Deployment of a gun in a crowded school being attacked by a shooter requires exceptional skill, judgment, and composure.

While there are far too many school shootings in the US relative to other countries, there are fewer than 50 per year in about 150,000 public and private schools or about 1 in every 3000 schools.[145] Just as in the case of firearms kept in the home, arming teachers in every school may well result in many more unforeseen misuses of firearms, including unauthorized uses of force, accidental shootings and discharges, and thefts of guns. Teachers may overreact in dealing with unruly students and use deadly force to control them, a departure from the intent of arming them. Issues relating to the disproportionate use of firearms against minority students may arise, as it is an issue with full-time, professionally trained law enforcement officers.[146]

Beefing up school security and arming school staff on a tight budget may marginally make schools safer, though the latter is fraught with perils and may even be counterproductive. This aside, these measures do nothing to address the reasons why so many young men in America wish to launch school attacks. Nor do these measures address the accessibility of weapons that enable these massacres. There is no low budget, quick fix to end school shootings. Unless schools are to become maximum security fortresses, we must address the factors that motivate shooters and provide easy access to weapons in the first place.

Recommendations for School Violence Prevention:

- Licensing gun owners would make it harder for those at risk of violence, but without felony records, to acquire firearms.

- Safe storage laws would make it harder for school shooters to obtain weapons from home or the residence of a relative or friend.

- Raising the age of all gun owners to 21 would mean that the many school shooters under that age could not acquire firearms legally.

- Encouraging the formation of peer groups in schools would help flag individuals who are struggling in school or socially and lead to the notification of officials if the peer group becomes aware of plans to commit violence.

- Tips from peers would be encouraged by positive interventions for troubled students rather than simply punitive interventions.

- Investments should be made to fund research and develop practices throughout the country that will reduce social isolation at all age levels.

- Building community networks can play an important role in reducing violence and self-injury. Governments at all levels should support the establishment of community structures and activities that promote the development of more involved, caring, and inclusive communities.

- Community-building initiatives should aim to prevent violence and to explore how to intervene when confronted with individuals who may be at risk of committing an act of extreme violence.

14

Lesson #2: The Availability of Lethal Methods Matters

The Case of Suicide

The World Health Organization considers suicide a form of self-directed violence. Regardless of whether we agree that suicide is a form of violence, the fact is that more than 20,000 Americans take their own lives with a firearm each year, and many of these deaths are preventable. Many members of the public believe that someone desiring to kill themselves will do so regardless of the methods available. They are incorrect. Leading experts tell us that just a small percentage of those who commit suicide (about 10 percent to 15 percent) had an unwavering desire to take their own lives. For the remainder, the risk is transient.[147]

There is a substantial body of evidence showing that many suicides have an impulsive component. Keith Hawton, a psychiatrist who heads Oxford University's Center for Suicide Research, has written about the issue of planning versus impulsivity in this ultimate act of self-harm:

> *For most people who become suicidal, the period of real risk is relatively brief, lasting in some individuals for even just a few minutes or a few hours. In others it may last days, but rarely longer. In some people, a lesser degree of risk is present for a much longer period of time, possibly years, and during that time they may go through periods of added and very high risk. The concept of periods of risk is very important in understanding the role of altering the availability of methods in prevention, in that if access to a dangerous means of suicide is restricted at such times, then survival until the end of these periods is more likely.[148]*

The Brady Center to Prevent Gun Violence similarly reports:

> *Various studies of survivors of suicide have calculated that as many as two-thirds of those who reported suicidal behavior did not plan their attempt. Interviews with survivors of near-lethal suicide attempts revealed that a quarter made the attempt less than five minutes after making the decision. About half of those did so within 20 minutes, and three-quarters of suicide attempts occurred within an hour. In a separate study, survivor interviews found that many made their attempt within 24 hours of a crisis, particularly interpersonal crises and physical fights.[149]*

A Texas study in the 1980s showed that suicidal thinking can be transient. The study examined the cases of 30 people who were treated for gunshot wounds to the head, chest, or abdomen.[150] Most, if not all, would have perished had a helicopter service and urban trauma center not been available. These were, therefore, very serious attempts.

Interviews revealed that half of these patients had been drinking within 24 hours of the suicide attempt and 18 of the 30 had experienced a significant interpersonal conflict during that period. Most had no longstanding psychiatric disorders, only two had a history of suicides, and none of the 30 left a suicide note. Half the patients reported having suicidal thoughts for less than 24 hours. Many expected to die from their attempt but indicated that they were glad to have survived. A follow-up two years later indicated that none had attempted suicide up to that point. This study showed that suicidal motivation can be fleeting yet very serious at the same time.

David Owens and his colleagues at the University of Leeds in the United Kingdom conducted a rigorous review of 90 research studies in which individuals who had attempted suicide and received medical care were followed up for one or more years.[151] The studies as a whole indicated that over two-thirds of suicide attempters were not known to have further attempts. Another 23 percent had an additional nonfatal attempt within four years. Two percent of the subjects across all the studies actually committed suicide within one year, and 7 percent of those monitored for nine years or more eventually committed suicide. Thus, one in every 14 people who attempted suicide once actually goes on to take his or her life.

Hawton of Oxford notes that the method of suicide may be more important to the outcome than the individual's intent. He writes:

> *Availability of a method may be the key factor that leads to translation of suicidal thoughts into an actual suicidal act.[152] Most importantly, the nature of the*

method that is available may have a vital influence on the outcome, particularly where an act is impulsive— then the person engaging in suicidal behavior is likely to use the means most easily available to them. If the method has a high risk of being fatal (e.g. firearms, highly toxic pesticides), then there is a strong possibility that the act will result in death.

Firearms have consistently been found to be the most lethal suicide method—85-90 percent of attempts are fatal.[153] The frequent impulsivity, ambivalence, and regret mean that the presence of lethal methods when an attempt is made may be all important in whether an individual succeeds in taking his life. There is abundant evidence that suicide methods are often chosen on the basis of their availability.

Many cases show that we cannot assume that people will switch to similarly lethal methods when their chosen method becomes unavailable. Therefore, much of what we know about suicide indicates that reducing access to highly lethal methods, such as firearms, is likely to lead to a reduction in suicides. It is important to note that many mass shooters and perpetrators of domestic killings are depressed and suicidal. Therefore, preventing suicidal actions may save the lives of others as well.

Recommendations:

- Individuals shown to be at a high risk for suicide, having a mental illness or a history of self-injury should be prohibited from acquiring or possessing firearms.

- Firearms should be stored securely to ensure that minors cannot obtain access to them.

- Safe storage and child access prevention laws should be enacted to keep firearms from minors who may be at risk of committing suicide.

- Firearms training should raise awareness of the impulsivity of many suicide attempts.

- Waiting periods for acquiring firearms or firearm licenses can prevent suicides.

- Red flag laws should authorize families and law enforcement to petition a court if they believe that an individual is at risk of suicide. Successful petitions should be promptly followed by the seizure of that individual's guns until professionals indicate that the crisis is over.

15

Concluding Remarks

America's unwillingness to address its gun violence problem is shameful. International human rights organizations, such as Amnesty International, have condemned the US for its failure to protect its citizens. The will of the majority of Americans who would like to see major solutions implemented should be respected. National policy should not be dictated by the National Rifle Association and a small minority of citizens who steadfastly refuse to compromise on this issue and who reject the idea that a balance must be struck between gun rights and public safety.

We owe it to the millions of children in America who are terrified to go to school and live in fear of mass and school shootings to do better. Our freedoms also are at stake as every atrocity leads to proposals to increase security and surveillance, to arm more civilians (e.g. teachers), and to conduct more invasive searches of our bodies and possessions. Unacceptable levels of violence also come at a high financial cost, including medical and rehabilitation costs, lost income, costs to the justice system, and the loss of business and tourism, as people go out less or decide against visiting places deemed to be too dangerous.

This book provides a road map in terms of solutions that are likely to make a difference given our current knowledge of gun violence. We have good ideas about what needs to be done, and public opinion has shifted decisively in favor of stricter gun regulation. More Americans are working on the ground as activists, and more political candidates are running on bold platforms that include significant reforms in gun policy. Following the mass shooting in Parkland, student leaders mobilized and inspired other young people to register to vote in record numbers.

More research is needed in this area, and private sources of funding and independent researchers have stepped up to fill the void created since the 1990s when Congressional Republicans, acting on behalf of the NRA, limited federal funding for gun violence research. A recent analysis showed that compared with other leading causes of death, gun violence was associated with far less funding and fewer publications than what would be predicted based on its associated mortality rate. About as many people die of gun violence as from sepsis; however, funding was less than 1 percent of that available for sepsis, and the volume of publications on gun violence was about 4 percent of the volume of reports on sepsis.[154]

Research is needed to gain a better understanding of guns in America, gun violence, and solutions that would prevent violence. Basic questions remain unanswered. There are gaps in regulations as well as in recordkeeping required when firearms are transferred. Information is needed to determine the number of guns in America, the number of assault-style weapons, and the volume of guns sold each year.

Other questions include: What types of guns are most likely to be used in crime? How many Americans own guns, and are stricter gun laws and lower levels of gun ownership associated with fewer gun deaths? What prevention and intervention strategies are most effective in reducing gun violence rates? In addition, the National Violent Death Reporting System should be expanded to all states to provide comprehensive national data on gun violence. Research is also needed to guide the assessment and identification of those at risk of violence and suicide.

The Centers for Disease Control and Prevention, National Institutes of Health, and National Institute of Justice should receive adequate funding to examine these outstanding questions. A periodic national survey should be conducted to determine the number of guns and gun owners in America (by county and state), the number of assault-style weapons and high-capacity magazines, and the prevalence of threats, assaults, suicides, and accidents with firearms. The survey also should obtain information on gun accessibility and storage.

We should never accept the large number of gun-related deaths and injuries as normal. We also need to remember that gun regulation has been present since the birth of America and usually has been far stricter. For example, in the second half of the 1800s, the carrying of concealed weapons was banned in most states.[155] Today, this practice is allowed in every state and treated as a right in most states. The notion that guns were carried with few restraints in the past is a fabrication propagated by advocates of gun rights. Also, guns are far more lethal today, and we must resist the fiction that they are beneficial to our society. The evidence to the contrary is overwhelming as more guns, more assault-style weapons, and the increasing carrying of guns for self-defense, along with enabling legislation like Stand Your Ground, brings only more violence.

The gun lobby's willful blindness with regard to the continuing parade of atrocities in America may be due to its cynical view that gun violence helps promote gun rights and sales in the name of self-protection. More gun ownership, however, only increases the level of violence. Public safety is not even a remote concern for the firearms industry, as demonstrated by their refusal to pass basic legislation that nine in 10 Americans (and even most gun owners) support.

The good news is that this lobby may be misjudging the American people as public attitudes shift in favor of stricter laws with each shooting, and more Americans become involved in the gun violence prevention movement. A growing number of Americans are saying, "Enough!"

POSTSCRIPT

A Declaration of Rights and Resolutions in Relation to Gun Violence

My previous book, *Confronting Gun Violence in America*, lays out the overwhelming evidence in support of basic gun regulation. While more research is needed, information to date shows that more gun ownership, carrying in public, and gun possession in the home is more likely to place people at risk than to serve as a deterrent to crime or a source of protection. Those favoring more restrictions on firearms have a much larger body of scientific research to draw on in debates than do those who favor expanding the rights of gun owners. However, when losing the evidence-based argument, gun rights advocates pull out their trump card: the Second Amendment of the US Constitution, which reads: "A well-regulated militia, being necessary to the security of a free state, the right of the people to keep and bear arms shall not be infringed."

Long interpreted by the higher courts as the right of citizens to form a militia, the landmark *Heller* decision by the US Supreme Court in 2008 interpreted the Second Amendment as conferring on Americans the right to possess a gun in the home for self-defense as opposed to militia service. Many gun owners believe incorrectly that this right is without limits and quickly move to a rights-based argument when the scientific merits of their arguments are weak. They will say something like, "Regardless of the research, the Constitution gives me a right to bear arms, period." Those seeking a safer society and reform of our gun laws at this point have no rights-based argument as a response and tend to get bogged down in a discussion of the meaning of the Second Amendment.

I believe it is time for the majority of Americans who are not gun owners, and the many owners who support reasonable controls on firearms, to develop their own Declaration of Rights to live free from violence. Such a Declaration would be consistent with the Declaration of Independence and human rights covenants. As pointed out by Amnesty International, personal safety is a human right. Currently, all Americans are vulnerable to gun violence, whether they live in large cities, small towns, or rural areas. There are few safe spaces in America given that so many venues have experienced mass shootings, including schools, college campuses, night clubs, theaters, libraries, airports, outdoor concerts, places of worship, shopping malls, baseball diamonds, newsrooms, and military bases.

I propose the following *Declaration of Rights and Resolutions in Relation to Gun Violence.*

Preamble

Whereas the United States is a signatory to the Universal Declaration of Human Rights which affirms that "Everyone has the right to life, liberty, and the security of person;"

Whereas Amnesty International has declared that the US government's refusal to pass gun control laws represents a violation of its citizens' rights to live free from violence and fear;

Whereas the Declaration of Independence affirms the right to life, liberty, and pursuit of happiness;

Whereas the US Constitution was established, in part, to "insure domestic Tranquility" and "promote the general Welfare;"

Whereas close to 40,000 Americans die and close to 100,000 suffer injuries from gunshot wounds each year;

Whereas many more Americans are traumatized and otherwise burdened by gun violence as witnesses, survivors, family members, and caregivers;

Whereas there is an average of about one civilian mass shooting a day in the United States;

Whereas mass shootings have occurred in schools, colleges, at night clubs and concerts, in movie theaters, places of worship, airports, workplaces, shopping malls, and elsewhere in our communities;

Whereas gun violence imposes heavy financial costs on individuals, our economy, and on our justice, medical, and educational systems;

Whereas high levels of gun violence and mass shootings reduce personal freedoms as they lead to intensified physical searches, policing, surveillance, and more records maintained on private citizens;

Whereas most citizens are not gun owners;

Whereas most Americans favor reasonable gun laws, such as universal background checks, bans on assault weapons and high-capacity magazines, and keeping guns from the mentally ill;

and,

Whereas the US Supreme Court ruled in 2008 (*District of Columbia v. Heller*) that the Second Amendment right is not unlimited and does not extend to the carrying of concealed weapons, possession of firearms by felons and the mentally ill, the carrying of firearms in sensitive places (e.g. schools and government buildings), or the carrying of dangerous or unusual weapons.

Therefore, this *Declaration* affirms that:

The People have the right to feel safe in their homes, at work, and in public spaces;

The People have the right to be in gun-free environments while in educational spaces;

The People have a First Amendment right to express their opinions on all subjects free of intimidation by citizens with guns;

The People have the right to move about, shop, work, and enjoy leisure activities in their communities without a fear of gun violence;

The People have the right to enjoy shows, sporting events, movies, and concerts without the presence of armed citizens (other than police) with guns;

The People have the right to use public transportation without the presence of citizens with guns;

The People have the right to attend church, temples,

mosques, and other places of worship without the presence of citizens with guns;

The People should be spared the physical harm, economic cost, and emotional trauma associated with gun violence.

Resolutions:

In order to safeguard the rights affirmed in this Declaration, the following policies should be pursued:

1. A national licensing system should be created for all gun owners, including interviews by law enforcement, a review of criminal and mental health records, reference checks, notification of spouses, gun safety training, and a waiting period.

2. Semiautomatic rifles with assault/military features and high-capacity magazines holding more than 10 rounds of ammunition should be banned or more strictly regulated. Devices that can increase the rate of fire of semiautomatic firearms (e.g. bump stocks) should be banned.

3. Gun carrying by the public in sensitive areas should be prohibited, including educational, cultural, religious, and sports facilities, public meetings, workplaces, and shopping malls unless a special exemption is obtained due to an imminent threat to a person's life.

4. Purchases by individuals should be limited to one firearm per month.

5. Personalized guns and safety features, such as loaded chamber indicators and magazine safeties, should

become manufacturing requirements and phased in over a short period of time.

6. Firearms should no longer be exempt from oversight by the Consumer Products Safety Commission. The *Protection of Lawful Commerce in Arms Act*, which shields gun manufacturers from liability for harm associated with their products, should be repealed.

7. The Bureau of Alcohol, Tobacco, Firearms and Explosives should have the authority and funding necessary to conduct inspections of gun dealers at its discretion as often as required.

8. Safe storage laws should be enacted to prevent suicides, accidents, and thefts while respecting the right of homeowners to possess a firearm for protection.

9. Laws enabling gun violence, such as Stand Your Ground, should be repealed.

10. A national research program should be created and funded in order to understand all aspects of gun violence, to prevent future violence, and to examine the impact of policies designed to reduce gun violence.

11. National standards should be developed regarding the use of force by police officers to prevent the shooting of unarmed civilians by the police. These standards should include sensitivity training to eliminate racial inequity and bias.

ENDNOTES

Preface

1 "Amnesty International, In the Line of Fire: Human Rights and the US Gun Violence Crisis." September 2018. Available at: https://www.amnesty.org.uk/files/2018-09/In%20the%20Line%20of%20Fire.pdf?1_qqjrC2Mv4H3YTt5TsdLepSKrgjKen0=

2 T. Smith and J. Son, "Trends in Gun Ownership in the United States," 1972-2014. Chicago: University of Chicago. National Opinion Research Center, 2015, p.1

Chapter 1

3 Melissa Healy, "Why the US is No. 1—in mass shootings." *LA Times* (August 24, 2015). Available at: http://www.latimes.com/science/sciencenow/la-sci-sn-united-states-mass-shooting-20150824-story.html

4 Erin Grinshteyn and David Hemenway, "Violent death rates: The US compared with other high income OECD countries," 2010. *The American Journal of Medicine*, 2016, 129: 266-73. Available at: https://www.amjmed.com/article/S0002-9343(15)01030-X/pdf

5 Chip Grabow and Lisa Rose, "The US had 57 times as many school shootings as the other major industrial nations combined." *CNN*

(May 21, 2018). Available at: https://www.cnn.com/2018/05/21/us/school-shooting-us-versus-world-trnd/index.html

6 Aaron Karp, "Estimating Global Civilian-Held Numbers. Small Arms Survey. Briefing paper" (June 2018). Available at: http://www.smallarmssurvey.org/fileadmin/docs/T-Briefing-Papers/SAS-BP-Civilian-Firearms-Numbers.pdf

7 S. Sorenson, "Guns in intimate partner violence: Comparing incidents by type of weapon." *Journal of Women's Health*, 2017, 26: 1-10

8 F. Norris, "Impact of mass shootings on survivors, families, and communities." *PTSD Research Quarterly*, 2007, 18: 1-8

9 American Psychological Association, "Stress in America: Generation Z." October 2018. Available at: https://www.apa.org/news/press/releases/stress/index.aspx

10 L. Qiu, "Number one cause of death among African American males 15-34 is murder." Politifact.com (August 2014). Available at: https://www.politifact.com/punditfact/statements/2014/aug/24/juan-williams/juan-williams-no-1-cause-death-african-americans-1/

11 T. Gabor, *Confronting Gun Violence in America*. London: Palgrave Macmillan, 2016, p.125

12 Marion Hammer, "It's time to name GOP betrayers who voted for Florida gun control." *AmmoLand* (April 18, 2018). Available at: https://www.ammoland.com/2018/04/its-time-to-name-gop-betrayers-who-voted-for-florida-gun-control/#axzz5D4EVj013

13 Laura Santhanam, "Poll: Gun control should be Congress' top priority, half of Americans say." PBS (April 19, 2018). Available at: https://www.pbs.org/newshour/politics/poll-gun-control-should-be-congress-top-priority-half-of-americans-say

14 N. Gonzalez, "Democratic candidates should be bolder on gun control, poll finds (August 1, 2018)." Available at: https://

www.rollcall.com/news/gonzales/democratic-candidates-bolder-gun-control-poll-finds

15 A. Samuels, "Gun owners and non-gun owners agree on many gun safety proposals." Johns Hopkins University (May 17, 2018). Available at: https://hub.jhu.edu/2018/05/17/gun-control-measures-gun-owners-survey/

16 D. Hakim and R. Shorey, "Gun control groups eclipse NRA in election spending." *New York Times* (November 16, 2018). Available at: https://www.nytimes.com/2018/11/16/us/politics/nra-gun-control-fund-raising.html

17 Giffords Law Center to Prevent Gun Violence, The Supreme Court and the Second Amendment. Available at: https://lawcenter.giffords.org/wp-content/uploads/2018/12/Supreme-Court-and-the-Second-Amendment-Factsheet.pdf

18 *District of Columbia et al. v. Heller* 554 U.S. 570 (2008). Supreme Court of the United States. Available at: http://www.supremecourt.gov/opinions/07pdf/07–290.pdf

19 T. Gabor, *Confronting Gun Violence in America*. London: Palgrave Macmillan, 2016.

20 M. Follman, J. Lurie, J. Lee, and J. West, "What does gun violence really cost?" Mother Jones (May/Jun 2015). Available at: http://www.motherjones.com/politics/2015/04/true-cost-of-gun-violence-in-america

Chapter 2

21 *Printz v. United States* 521 US 898 (1997).

22 US Government Accountability Office, "Gun Control: Sharing Promising Practices and Assessing Incentives Could Better Position Justice to Assist States in Providing Records for Background Checks" (July, 16, 2012). Available at: https://www.gao.gov/products/GAO-12-68

23 Giffords Law Center to Prevent Gun Violence, NICS and

Reporting Procedure. Available at: https://lawcenter.giffords. org/gun-laws/policy-areas/background-checks/nics-reporting-procedures/

24 *Everytown for Gun Safety*, "Fatal Gaps: How missing records in the federal background check system put guns in the hands of killers." Available at: https://everytownresearch.org/ reports/fatal-gaps/

25 K. Kennedy, "Disturbing Instagram posts: What Nikolas Cruz, suspected in Florida shooting, did online." *USA Today* (February 15, 2018). Available at: https://www.usatoday.com/ story/news/2018/02/15/nikolas-cruz-who-florida-shooting-suspect-social-media/340092002/

26 Matt Stevens, "Judge rebukes FBI over how killer got his gun." *New York Times* (June 21, 2018), p. A16.

27 Ladd Everitt, "Background checks on gun buyers were designed to fail—by the NRA." *Medium* (May 29, 2018). Available at: https://medium.com/@LaddEveritt/background-checks-on-gun-buyers-were-designed-to-fail-by-the-nra-b2d4a66afbda

28 Quoted in Everitt, "Background checks on gun buyers were designed to fail—by the NRA."

29 Steve Contorno, "Adam Putnam blamed one employee for bungling gun background checks. Records show the issue went deeper." *Tampa Bay Times* (July 6, 2018). Available at: https:// www.tampabay.com/florida-politics/buzz/2018/07/06/adam-putnam-blamed-one-employee-for-bungling-gun-background-checks-records-show-the-issue-went-deeper/?template=amp

30 Mike Weisser, "Do comprehensive background checks reduce gun violence? Not so far." *Mikethegunguy.com: A Magazine with News and Notes About Guns* (August 3, 2018). Available at: https://mikethegunguy.com/2018/08/03/do-comprehensive-background-checks-reduce-gun-violence-not-so-far/

31 Cassandra Crifasi, Molly Merrill-Francis, Alex McCourt, Jon Vernick, Garen Wintemute, and Daniel Webster, "Association between firearm laws and homicide in urban counties." *Science Daily* (May 31, 2018). Available at: https://www.sciencedaily. com/releases/2018/05/180531171607.htm;

Chapter 3

32 Crime Prevention Research Center, "New study: Over 14.5 million concealed handgun permits; last year saw the largest increase ever in the number of permits" (July 26, 2016). Available at: https://crimeresearch.org/2016/07/new-study-14-5-million-concealed-handgun-permits-last-year-saw-largest-increase-ever-number-permits/

33 T. Gabor, "Congress is about to let people carry guns anywhere in the US." *Fortune* (December 5, 2017). Available at: http://fortune.com/2017/12/05/concealed-carry-reciprocity-act-hr-38-gun-control/

34 R. Spitzer, "Stand Your Ground Makes No Sense." *The New York Times* (May 15, 2015). Available from: https://www.nytimes. com/2015/05/04/opinion/stand-your-ground-makes-no-sense.html

35 M. Martinovich, "States with right-to-carry concealed handgun laws experience increases in violent crime, according to Stanford scholar." *Stanford News* (June 21, 2017). Available at: https://news.stanford.edu/2017/06/21/violent-crime-increases-right-carry-states/

36 Federal Bureau of Investigation, "A study of Active Shooter Incidents in the United States Between 2000 and 2013." Washington, DC: US Department of Justice, 2014

37 J. Kay, "More guns aren't the answer. For Canadians, America's gun cult looks like a collective suicide cult." *National Post* (January 8, 2016). Available at: http://news.nationalpost. com/full-comment/jonathankay-more-guns-arent-the-answer-americans-are-likelier-to-wet-theirpants-facing-a-mass-shooter

38 J. Vince, T. Wolfe, L. Field, Firearms training and self-defense. Chicago: National Gun Victims Action Council; 2015. P. 4

39 Violence Policy Center, Concealed Carry Killers. Available at: http://concealedcarrykillers.org/

40 T. Gabor, *Confronting Gun Violence in America*, p.169

41 Giffords Law Center to Prevent Gun Violence, "Concealed Carry." Available at: http://lawcenter.giffords.org/gun-laws/policy-areas/guns-in-public/concealed-carry/

42 T. Gabor, *Confronting Gun Violence in America*, p.237

43 J. Holland, "Tactical experts destroy the NRA's heroic gunslinger fantasy." *The Nation* (October 5, 2015). Available at: http://www.thenation.com/article/combat-vets-destroy-the-nras-heroic-gunslinger-fantasy/

44 Holland J. "Tactical experts destroy NRA's gunslinger fantasy."

45 Dahl J. "Empire State Building shooting sparks questions about NYPD shot accuracy." *CBS News* (August 29, 2012). Available at: http://www.cbsnews.com/8301-504083_162-57502545-504083/empire-state-buildingshooting-sparks-questions-about-nypd-shot-accuracy/

46 Vince et al., *Firearms training and self-defense.* P. 19

47 J. Mascia, "26 states will let you carry a concealed gun without making sure you know how to shoot one." *The Trace* (February 2, 2016). Available at: https://www.thetrace.org/2016/02/live-fire-training-not-mandatory-concealed-carry-permits/

48 Florida Department of Agriculture and Consumer Services Division of Licensing. Available at: https://www.freshfromflorida.com/content/download/82618/2393451/Number_of_Licensees_By_Type.pdf

49 *District of Columbia v. Heller* 554 U.S. 570 (2008)

Chapter 4

50 American Psychological Association. "Gun violence: prediction, prevention, and policy." Washington, DC: Public and Member Communications, 2013, P. 4

51 The Educational Fund to Stop Gun Violence, "Domestic Violence and Guns in the United States: A Lethal Combination" (October 2016)

52 J. Swanson, N. Sampson, M. Petukhova, A. Zaslavsky, P. Appelbaum, M. Swartz, "Guns, impulsive angry behavior, and mental disorders: Results from the National Comorbidity Survey Replication (NCS-R)." *Behavioral Science and Law*, 2015; 33(2–3): 199–212

53 B. Vossekuil, R. Fein, M. Reddy, R. Borum, and W. Modzelewski, "The Final Report and Findings of the Safe School Initiative: Implications for the Prevention of School Attacks in the United States." Washington, DC: United States Secret Service and the United States Department of Education; 2004

54 James Silver, Andre Simons, and Sarah Craun, "A Study of the Pre-Attack Behaviors of Active Shooters in the United States," Federal Bureau of Investigation, June 2018, https://www.fbi.gov/file-repository/pre-attack-behaviors-of-active-shooters-in-us-2000-2013.pdf/view

55 Aaron J. Kivisto and Peter Lee Phalen, "Effects of Risk-Based Firearm Seizure Laws in Connecticut and Indiana on Suicide Rates, 1981–2015." *Psychiatric Services* (2018)

56 Giffords Law Center to Prevent Gun Violence, Extreme Risk Protection Orders. Available at: http://lawcenter.giffords.org/gun-laws/policy-areas/who-can-have-a-gun/extreme-risk-protection-orders/

Chapter 5

57 B. Vossekuil, R. Fein, M. Reddy, R. Borum, W. Modzelewski, "The Final Report and Findings of the Safe School Initiative: Implications for the Prevention of School Attacks in the United States." Washington, DC: United States Secret Service and the United States Department of Education; 2002

58 M. Shuster, T. Franke, A. Bastian, S. Sor, N. Halfon, "Firearm storage patterns in US Homes with children." *American Journal of Public Health.* 2000; 90(4): 588–594

59 C. Crifasi et al., "Survey: More than half of US gun owners do not safely store their guns." *Johns Hopkins Bloomberg School of Public Health* (February 22, 2018). Available at: https://www.jhsph.edu/news/news-releases/2018/survey-more-than-half-of-u-s-gun-owners-do-not-safely-store-their-guns.html

60 F. Baxley, M. Miller, "Parental Misperceptions About Children and Firearms." *Archives of Pediatric & Adolescent Medicine*, 2006, 160: 542–547

61 A. Yablon, "Roughly 400 Americans will die in unintentional home shootings this year. Safe storage laws aim to lower that number." *The Trace* (September 30, 2015). Available at: https://www.thetrace.org/2015/09/safe-storage-gun-la-san-francisco-nyc-accidental-shooting/

62 US General Accounting Office. "Accidental Shootings: Many Deaths and Injuries Caused by Firearms Could be Prevented." Washington, DC: US General Accounting Office; 1991.

63 Rand Corporation, "Gun Policy in America: An Overview" (2018). Available at: https://www.rand.org/research/gun-policy/essays/gun-policy-in-america.html

64 Children's National Health System. "Stricter state firearms laws associated with lower pediatric mortality rates from firearms: Pediatric providers could play pivotal roles in

educating parents about pediatric firearm safety." *ScienceDaily.* (May 5, 2018). Available at: https://www.sciencedaily.com/releases/2018/05/180505091819.htm

65 American Academy of Pediatrics Committee on Adolescence. "Firearms and adolescents." *Pediatrics*, 1992, 89(4): 784–787

66 C. Barry, E. McGinty, J. Vernick, D. Webster, "After Newtown—public opinion on gun policy and mental illness." *New England Journal of Medicine*, 2013, 368: 1077-1081

67 Giffords Law Center to Prevent Gun Violence, "Safe Storage." Available at: http://lawcenter.giffords.org/gun-laws/policy-areas/child-consumer-safety/safe-storage/

68 R. Gebelhoff, "Gun reforms can save lives. Science proves it." *Washington Post* (March 23, 2018). Available at: https://www.washingtonpost.com/classic-apps/gun-reforms-can-save-lives-science-proves-it/2018/03/23/d7403cb2-2891-11e8-874b-d517e912f125_story.html?utm_term=.258728908c5d

69 "Seattle City Council passes resolution that would levy fines for unlocked guns." *KOMOnews.com* (July 9, 2018). Available at: http://komonews.com/news/local/proposed-seattle-ordinance-would-levy-fines-for-unlocked-gun

70 Rand Corporation, "The Science of Gun Policy." Santa Monica, Cal.: Rand, 2018

71 Personal communication with Barbara Markley

Chapter 6

72 Everytown for Gun Safety. "Analysis of Recent Mass Shootings." New York, 2015.

73 Christopher Koper, William Johnson, Jordan Nichols, Ambrozine Ayers, and Natalie Mullins, "Criminal use of assault weapons and high-capacity semiautomatic firearms: An updated examination of local and national sources." *Journal of Urban Health.* Published online on October 2, 2017

74 Gabor, *Confronting Gun Violence in America*, Chapter 5

75 M. Roth, "Gunshot wound care has improved dramatically." *Pittsburgh Post-Gazette*. (Jul. 23, 2012). Available at: http://www.postgazette.com/stories/news/health/gunshot-wound-care-has-improveddramatically-645837/#ixzz2hnldZnfn

76 A. Yablon, "Bullets per body rise in Chicago as high-capacity handguns gain criminal following." *The Trace* (January 2, 2018). Available at: https://www.thetrace.org/rounds/chicago-multiple-gunshots-high-capacity-handguns/

77 Gina Kolata and C.J. Chivers, "Wounds from military-style rifles: A 'ghastly thing to see.'" *New York Times* (March 4, 2018). Available at: https://www.nytimes.com/2018/03/04/health/parkland-shooting-victims-ar15.html

78 Heather Sher, "What I saw treating the victims from Parkland should change the debate on guns." *The Atlantic* (February 22, 2018). Available at: https://www.theatlantic.com/politics/archive/2018/02/what-i-saw-treating-the-victims-from-parkland-should-change-the-debate-on-guns/553937/?utm_source=atlfb;

79 C. Koper, "America's experience with the federal assault weapons ban," 1994–2004. In: D. Webster and J. Vernick, editors. *Reducing Gun Violence in America: Informing Policy with Evidence and Analysis*. Baltimore: Johns Hopkins University Press; 2013, P. 159–160.

80 Louis Klarevas, *Rampage Nation: Securing America from Mass Shootings*. New York: Penguin Random House, 2016.

81 Australian Institute of Criminology. Legislative reforms. Available at: http://www.aic.gov.au/publications/current%20series/rpp/100-120/rpp116/06_reforms.html

82 Philip Alpers, "The big melt: how one democracy changed after scrapping a third of its firearms." In: Webster D, Vernick J, editors. *Reducing Gun Violence in America*. Baltimore: The Johns Hopkins University Press; 2013

83 S. Chapman, P. Alpers, K. Agho, M. Jones, "Australia's 1996 gun law reforms: Faster falls in firearm deaths, firearm suicides, and a decade without mass shootings." *Injury Prevention*, 2006; 12(6): 365–372

84 ATF, National Firearms Act. Available at: https://www.atf. gov/rules-and-regulations/national-firearms-act

85 Bureau of Alcohol, Tobacco, Firearms and Explosives, *Firearms Commerce in the United States: Annual Statistical Update*, 2017, Exhibit 8. Available at: https://www.atf.gov/resource-center/docs/undefined/firearms-commerce-united-states-annual-statistical-update-2017/download

86 A. Yablon, "Most Californians who own 'assault rifles' have 10+ guns." *The Trace* (November 12, 2018). Available at: https:// www.thetrace.org/rounds/california-assault-rifle-ownership-gun-super-owners/

Chapter 7

87 National Physicians Alliance, *Gun Safety and Public Health*. August, 2013, p.10

88 C. Bettigole, "Guns, public health, and the Consumer Products Safety Commission." *Washington, DC: National Physicians Alliance* (May 25, 2013). Available at: http:// npalliance.org/blog/2013/05/25/guns-public-health-and-the-consumer-products-safety-commission/

89 J. Vernick, M. O'Brien, L. Hepburn, S. Johnson, D. Webster, S. Hargarten, "Unintentional and undetermined firearm-related deaths: a preventable death analysis for three safety devices." *Injury Prevention*, 2003, 9(4): 307–311

90 M. Greene, "A Review of Gun Safety Technologies." *Washington, DC: National Institute of Justice*, 2013

91 "Attorney General's Report to the Governor and the

Legislature as to the Availability of Personalized Handguns for Retail Sales Purposes, Pursuant to N.J.S. 2C: 58-2.3" (November 2014). Available at: http://www.njleg.state.nj.us/opi/Reports_to_the_Legislature/attorney_general_personalized_handgun_retail_report_Nov_2014.pdf

92 Katie Trumbly, "Why the NRA opposes smart guns" (October 15, 2014). Available at: https://www.highbrowmagazine.com/4363-why-nra-opposes-smart-guns

Chapter 8

93 B. Freskos, "A New Generation of Entrepreneurs Thinks It Can Revive the Smart Gun." *The Trace* (January 21, 2019). Available at: https://www.thetrace.org/2019/01/a-new-generation-of-entrepreneurs-thinks-it-can-revive-the-smart-gun/

94 Brady Campaign to Prevent Gun Violence, *The Protection of Lawful Commerce in Arms Act (PLCAA)*. Available at: http://www.bradycampaign.org/the-protection-of-lawful-commerce-in-arms-act-plcaa

95 Nicholas Kristof, "How to reduce shootings." *New York Times* (May 18, 2018). Available at: https://www.nytimes.com/interactive/2017/11/06/opinion/how-to-reduce-shootings.html

96 Amanda Marcotte, "Could suing the gun industry begin to stem the bloodshed." *Salon.com* (October 4, 2017). Available at: https://www.salon.com/2017/10/04/could-suing-the-gun-industry-begin-to-stem-the-bloodshed/

97 US Environmental Protection Agency, "What is superfund?" Available at: https://www.epa.gov/superfund/what-superfund

98 A. Yablon, "New York hits 10 more insurers with millions in fines for underwriting NRA policies." *The Trace* (December 21, 2018). Available at: https://www.thetrace.org/rounds/new-york-hits-ten-more-insurers-with-millions-in-fines-for-underwriting-nra-policies/

99 Bureau of Alcohol, Tobacco, Firearms and Explosives. "Commerce in Firearms in the United States." Washington, DC: US Department of the Treasury, 2000

Chapter 9

100 D. Hennigan, *Lethal Logic*. Washington, DC: Potomac Books, 2009, pp. 174–175

101 Bureau of Alcohol, Tobacco, Firearms and Explosives. "Following the gun: Enforcing federal law against firearms traffickers." Washington, DC: US Department of the Treasury; 2000.

102 The City of New York. "Gun Show Undercover: Report on Illegal Sales at Gun Shows." New York: The City of New York; 2009

103 "ABC News. Guns in America: A Statistical Look." *ABC News* (August 25, 2012). Available at: http://abcnews.go.com/blogs/headlines/2012/08/guns-in-america-a-statistical-look/

104 B. Siebel, E. Haile, "Shady dealings: illegal gun trafficking from licensed dealers." Washington, DC: Brady Center to Prevent Gun Violence; 2007, P. 24

105 Office of the Inspector General. "Inspections of Firearm Dealers by the Bureau of Alcohol, Tobacco, Firearms and Explosives." Washington, DC: US Department of Justice, 2004. P. iii.

106 S. Horwitz, J. Grimaldi, "ATF's oversight limited in face of gun lobby." *Washington Post* (October 26, 2010). Available at: http://www.washingtonpost.com/wp-dyn/content/article/2010/10/25/AR2010102505823.html?sub=AR

107 Bureau of Alcohol, Tobacco and Firearms. "Gun Shows: Brady Checks and Crime Gun Traces." Washington, DC: Department of the Treasury and Department of Justice, 1999.

108 Bureau of Alcohol, Tobacco and Firearms. *Gun Shows*. P. 6.

109 N. Kristof, "Lessons from the Virginia shooting." *The New York Times* (August 26, 2015). Available at: http://www.nytimes.com/2015/08/27/opinion/lessons-from-the-murders-of-tvjournalists-in-the-virginia-shooting.html?smid=nytcore-ipad-share&smprod=nytcore-ipad&_r=1

110 *Mayors Against Illegal Guns.* "Trace the Guns: The link Between Gun Laws and Interstate Gun Trafficking." New York: Mayors Against Illegal Guns, 2010.

111 I. Irvin, K. Rhodes, R. Cheney, D. Wiebe, "Evaluating the effect of state regulation of federally licensed firearm dealers on firearm homicide." *American Journal of Public Health.* 2014; 104(8): 1384–1386

112 D. Webster, J. Vernick, "Spurring responsible firearms sales practices through litigation." In: D. Webster, J. Vernick, editors. *Reducing Gun Violence in America.* Baltimore: Johns Hopkins University Press; 2013, pp.123–31.

Chapter 10

113 K. Hundley, S. Martin, C. Humburg, "Florida 'Stand Your Ground' law yields some shocking outcomes depending on how law is applied." *Tampa Bay Times* (June 1, 2012). Available at: http://www.tampabay.com/news/publicsafety/crime/florida-stand-your-ground-law-yields-some-shockingoutcomes-depending-on/1233133

114 B. Montgomery, C. Jenkins, "Five years since Florida enacted "Stand Your Ground' law, justifiable homicides are up." *Tampa Bay Times* (October 15, 2010). Available at: http://www.tampabay.com/news/publicsafety/crime/five-years-since-florida-enacted-stand-your-groundlaw-justifiable/1128317

115 D. Humphreys, A. Gasparrini, D. Wiebe, "Evaluating the impact of Florida's 'Stand Your Ground' self-defense law on homicide and suicide by firearm: An interrupted time series study." *JAMA Internal Medicine*, 2017, 177: 44-50. Available at: https://www.ncbi.nlm.nih.gov/pubmed/27842169

116 C. Parsons, E. Vargas, "The Devastating Impact of Stand Your Ground in Florida." Center for American Progress (2018). Available at: https://www.americanprogressaction.org/issues/guns-crime/news/2018/10/17/172031/devastating-impact-stand-ground-florida/

117 C. Cheng, M. Hoekstra, "Does strengthening self-defense law deter crime or escalate violence?" *The Journal of Human Resources*, 2013, 48: 821-853. Available at: http://business.baylor.edu/Scott_Cunningham/teaching/cheng-and-hoekstra-2013.pdf

118 American Bar Association, *National Task Force on Stand Your Ground Laws. Preliminary Report and Recommendations*, pp. 21–22.

Chapter 11

119 National Institute of Justice, Focused Deterrence Programs. Available at: https://www.crimesolutions.gov/PracticeDetails.aspx?ID=11

120 D. Kennedy, A. Braga, A. Piehl, "The (un)known universe: mapping gangs and gang violence in Boston." In: D. Weisburd, J. McEwen, editors. *Crime Mapping and Crime Prevention*. Monsey, NY: Criminal Justice Press, 1997, pp. 219–262.

121 A. Braga, D. Weisburd, "Focused deterrence and the prevention of violent gun injuries: practice, theoretical principles, and scientific evidence." *Annual Review of Public Health*, 2015, 36: 55–68

122 National Institute of Justice, *Program Profile—Police Foot Patrol—Philadelphia 2009*. Available at: https://www.crimesolutions.gov/ProgramDetails.aspx?ID=234

123 M. Obbie, "The wonks guide to what works and what doesn't, when policing violent crime." *The Trace* (August 11, 2016). Available at: https://www.thetrace.org/2016/08/policing-tactics-what-works/

124 J. Butts, C. Roman, L. Bostwick, J. Porter, "Cure violence: A public health model to reduce gun violence." *Annual Review of Public Health*, 2015, 36: 39-53.

Chapter 12

125 B. Vossekuil, R. Fein, M. Reddy, R. Borum, W. Modzeleski, *The Final Report and Findings of the Safe School Initiative: Implications for the Prevention of School Attacks in the United States*. Washington, DC: United States Secret Service and the United States Department of Education, 2002.

126 K. Masters, "Police trade cash for thousands of guns each year. But experts say it does little to stem violence." *The Trace* (July 17, 2015). Available at: https://www.thetrace.org/2015/07/gun-buyback-study-effectivness/

127 M. Burgos, "Deputies receive more than 1,100 guns at gun swap event." *ABC Action News* (October 6, 2018). Available at: https://www.abcactionnews.com/news/deputies-receive-more-than-1-100-guns-at-gun-swap-event?autoplay=true

128 K. Snyder, "Mayor: Toledo will only buy from responsible gun companies." *The Blade* (October 30, 2018). Available at: https://www.toledoblade.com/local/police-fire/2018/10/30/mayor-toledo-will-only-buy-from-responsible-gun-companies/stories/20181030112

129 R. Dyer, "Academe versus US gun culture." *Inside Higher Ed* (March 29, 2018). Available at: https://www.insidehighered.com/views/2018/03/29/growing-movement-divest-gun-manufacturers-opinion

130 J. Schuppe, "How a Seattle nun led a shareholder revolt against gun makers." *NBC News* (September 30, 2018). Available at: https://www.nbcnews.com/news/us-news/how-seattle-nun-led-shareholder-revolt-against-gun-makers-n915006

131 "Reach Beyond Domestic Violence, History." Available at: https://reachma.org/who-we-are/history/

132 N. Gonzales, "Democratic candidates should be bolder on gun control, poll finds." *Roll Call* (August 1, 2018). Available at: https://www.rollcall.com/news/gonzales/democratic-candidates-bolder-gun-control-poll-finds

133 J. Rose, B. Booker, "Parkland shooting suspect: A story of red flags ignored." *NPR* (March 1, 2018). Available at: https://www.npr.org/2018/02/28/589502906/a-clearer-picture-of-parkland-shooting-suspect-comes-into-focus

134 *Sandy Hook Promise*, "Know the signs programs." Available at: https://www.sandyhookpromise.org/prevention_ programs

Chapter 13

135 C. Grabow and L. Rose, "The US has had 57 times as many school shootings as the other industrialized nations combined." *CNN* (May 21, 2018). Available at: https://www.cnn.com/2018/05/21/us/school-shooting-us-versus-world-trnd/index.html

136 US Secret Service and Department of Education, *The Final Report and Findings of the Safe School Initiative.* Available at: http://www.scstatehouse.gov/CommitteeInfo/SchoolSafetyTaskForce/September112014Meeting/ssi_final_report.pdf

137 R. Putnam, *Bowling Alone: The Collapse and Revival of American Community.* New York: Simon and Shuster, 2000.

138 D. Grossman, "Reducing youth firearm suicide risk." *Pediatrics.* Published online, February 21, 2018.

139 B. Vossekuil et al., *The Final Report and Findings of the Safe School Initiative.* P. 22.

140 J. Cox, S. Rich, "School shootings: Should parents be charged for failing to lock up guns used by their kids?" *Washington Post* (August 1, 2018). Available at: https://www.washingtonpost.

com/news/local/wp/2018/08/01/feature/school-shootings-should-parents-be-charged-for-failing-to-lock-up-guns-used-by-their-kids/?utm_term=.6de65b5ffd92--70%

141 A. Moore, "Chicago dropout reengagement centers part of a growing national trend." *National League of Cities* (August 8, 2013). Available at: http://www.nlc.org/media-center/news-search/chicago-dropout-reengagementcenters-part-of-a-growing-national-trend

142 National Education Association. "Combating social isolation: It starts with hello" (February 18, 2016). Available at: http://www.learningfirst. org/combatting-social-isolation-it-starts-hello

143 Quinnipiac University Poll, "Florida voters oppose teachers with guns" (February 28, 2018). Available at: https://poll.qu.edu/florida/release-detail?ReleaseID=2524

144 M. Hiltzik, "One big problem with the idea of arming teachers: Insurance companies won't play along, and for good reason." *LA Times* (February 26, 2018). Available at: http://www.latimes.com/business/hiltzik/la-fi-hiltzik-arming-teachers-20180226-story.html

145 J. Patel, "After Sandy Hook: More than 400 people have been shot in over 200 school shootings." *NY Times* (February 15, 2018). Available at: https://www.nytimes.com/interactive/2018/02/15/us/school-shootings-sandy-hook-parkland.html

146 M. Martinez, "Arming teachers only creates more problems." *The Daily Northwestern* (February 25, 2018). Available at: https://dailynorthwestern.com/2018/02/25/lateststories/martinez-arming-teachers-creates-problems/

Chapter 14

147 K. Jamison, *Night Falls Fast: Understanding Suicide*. New York: Knopf, 1999. P. 47.

148 K. Hawton, "Restriction of access to methods of suicide as a means of suicide prevention." In: K. Hawton, editor. *Prevention and treatment of suicidal behavior: from science to practice.* Oxford: Oxford University Press, 2005. Pp. 283-284

149 The Brady Center to Prevent Gun Violence. "The Truth About Suicide and Guns." Washington, DC: The Brady Center to Prevent Gun Violence, 2015. P. 10.

150 L. Peterson, M. Peterson, G. O'Shanick, A. Swann, "Self-inflicted gunshot wounds: lethality of method versus intent." *American Journal of Psychiatry*, 1985, 142(2): 228–231

151 D. Owens, J. Horrocks, A. "House, Fatal and non-fatal repetition of self harm: systematic review." *British Journal of Psychiatry*, 2002, 181(3): 193–199.

152 K. Hawton, "Restriction of access to methods of suicide as a means of suicide prevention." P. 279

153 T. Gabor, *Confronting Gun Violence in America*, pp. 94-95.

154 D. Stark, N. Shah, "Funding and publication of research on gun violence and other leading causes of death." *Journal of the American Medical Association*, 2017, 317: 84-85. Available at: https://jamanetwork.com/journals/jama/fullarticle/2595514

155 Gabor, *Confronting Gun Violence in America*, Chapter 1

CPSIA information can be obtained
at www.ICGtesting.com
Printed in the USA
BVHW031725031219
565540BV00001B/43/P